READINGS IN SRI AUROBINDO'S
THE SYNTHESIS OF YOGA

VOL. 3

The Yoga of Divine Love

Santosh Krinsky

PO Box 325
Twin Lakes, WI

Chapter Numbers and Titles follow the original text of *The Synthesis of Yoga*; however, the sub-titles of the summary and interpretation of the chapters are entirely those of the author.

ISBN: 978-0-9406-7643-5

Library of Congress Number: 2015952802

Published by:

LOTUS
PRESS

Lotus Press
P.O. Box 325
Twin Lakes, WI 53181 USA
800-824-6396 (toll free order phone)
262-889-8561 (office phone)
262-889-2461 (office fax)
www.lotuspress.com (website)
lotuspress@lotuspress.com (email)

Printed In USA

TABLE OF CONTENTS

DEDICATION AND ACKNOWLEDGEMENTS

I dedicate this book to Sri Aurobindo and the Mother, who have guided and blessed my life and seeking for all of my adult life.

I would like to acknowledge also a debt of gratitude to Sri M.P. Pandit, who taught by example and by his tremendous discipline and dedication to the yoga of Sri Aurobindo and the Mother. I was particularly inspired to follow the current book's format from his *Readings in Savitri* (10 volume set) which encouraged me to dedicate time regularly over a period of years to carry out the process of creating these readings.

I am grateful to my life-partner and wife Karuna who has been a support and inspiration to me with her quiet and dedicated efforts of sadhana, as well as to my two children Marina Mahati and Shanta Maya who challenged us to grow and expand our view of life as we raised and home-schooled them.

I have to also acknowledge the efforts of His Holiness, the XIV Dalai Lama, whose compassionate, caring and tireless efforts for building a world of peace, harmony and understanding have provided support and solace in a world filled with conflict and suffering.

INTRODUCTION

INTRODUCTION TO SRI AUROBINDO'S THE SYNTHESIS OF YOGA

In *The Synthesis of Yoga* Sri Aurobindo unfolds his vision of an integral (also called "purna" or "complete") yoga embracing all the powers and activities of man. He provides an overview of the main paths of yoga, their primary methodologies and the necessity for integrating them into a complete, all-embracing and all-encompassing activity. The motto "All Life Is Yoga" is the theme of this text.

Sri Aurobindo points out that this is not intended as a fixed methodology: "*The Synthesis of Yoga* was not meant to give a method for all to follow. Each side of the Yoga was dealt with separately with all its possibilities, and an indication as to how they meet so that one starting from knowledge could realise Karma and Bhakti also and so with each path." (pg. 899)

The final section begins to flesh out an integrative method which Sri Aurobindo called the "yoga of self-perfection". While all the details of this approach were not completed to the extent desired, Sri Aurobindo has provided ample guidelines for the seeker to understand the direction and the path.

It is our goal to take up the systematic review of *The Synthesis of Yoga* in the following pages.

All page number citations in this review are based on the U.S. edition of *The Synthesis of Yoga* published by Lotus Press, EAN: 978-0-9415-2465-0 Sri Aurobindo,The Synthesis of Yoga.

Chapter headings and organization of the material follow *The Synthesis of Yoga;* however, the sub-titles of the summary and interpretation of the chapters are entirely those of the author.

PART III
THE YOGA OF DIVINE LOVE

Chapter One

Love and the Triple Path

The Union of Will, Knowledge and Love in God

The various paths of realization each begin from one major power within the human being, whether it be the path of works, the path of knowledge or the path of love and devotion. One can view the rise of spiritual and religious traditions throughout the world with this lens and see that they tend to fit, more or less cleanly, into one or the other of these three frames. In many cases, the adherents of one path or religion tend to conflate their own methodology with being the only true method, and they then may tend to either denigrate or look down upon the adherents of other ways. In the end, however, it becomes clear that an integral realization must eventually recognize the bona fide importance of each of these three major streams of growth into the divine status.

Sri Aurobindo observes: "The integrality of them, the union of man with God in all the three, must therefore, as we have seen, be the foundation of an integral Yoga."

Due to the need for action in life, will in works is the general first phase of the spiritual development: "When the will in him is made one with the divine will and the whole action of the being proceeds from the Divine and is directed towards the Divine, the union in works is perfectly accomplished. But works fulfil themselves in knowledge; all the totality of works, says the Gita, finds its rounded culmination in knowledge.... By union in will and works we become one in the omnipresent conscious being from whom all our will and works have their rise and draw their power and in whom they fulfil the round of their energies. And the crown of this union is love; for love is the delight of conscious union with the Being in whom we live, act and move, by whom we exist, for whom alone we learn in the end to act and to be. That is the trinity of our powers, the union of all three in God to which we arrive when we start from works as our way of access and our line of contact."

From whichever aspect one begins, eventually the three draw together in the integral fulfilment.

Sri Aurobindo, The Synthesis of Yoga, Part Three: The Yoga of Divine Love, Chapter 1, Love and the Triple Path, pg. 521

The Union of Knowledge With Will and Divine Love

For the seeker who takes up the path of Knowledge, there comes a time when the aspects of Will and Divine Love join to enhance and complete the practice. Sri Aurobindo reminds us that: "The Divine meets us in many aspects and to each of them knowledge is the key, so that by knowledge we enter into and possess the infinite and Divine in every way of our being, *sarvabhavena* (Gita), and receive him into us and are possessed by him in every way of ours."

The Knowledge referred to here is not some kind of intellectual knowing, not, in fact, what we consider to be knowledge in our various educational systems. Rather, Knowledge is something acquired through Oneness with the object of knowledge, in this case, the Divine Being. That Oneness provides us with "knowledge by identity" which does not require words to understand or explain itself. "But knowledge is not complete without works; for the Will in being also is God and not the being or its self-aware silent existence alone, and if works finds their culmination in knowledge, knowledge also finds its fulfilment in works."

"And, here too, love is the crown of knowledge; for love is the delight of union, and unity must be conscious of joy of union to find all the riches of its own delight. Perfect knowledge indeed leads to perfect love, integral knowledge to a rounded and multitudinous richness of love."

" 'He who knows me,' says the Gita, 'as the supreme Purusha',–not only as the immutable oneness, but in the many-souled movement of the Divine and as that, superior to both, in which both are divinely held,– 'he, because he has the integral knowledge, seeks me by love in every way of his being.' "

"This is the trinity of our powers, the union of all three in God to which we arrive when we start from knowledge."

Sri Aurobindo, The Synthesis of Yoga, Part Three: The Yoga of Divine Love, Chapter 1, Love and the Triple Path, pp. 521-522

The Union of Divine Love
With Knowledge and Will

There is something of a misconception that the path of devotion does not require nor develop the powers of Knowledge or Will. The devotional merging of the personality brings the ecstasy of union and it is easy to overlook the deeper spiritual significance that brings everything else with it when the devotion becomes complete.

In the Taittiriya Upanishad, as the seeker evolves in his understanding about the cause and foundation of the universe, eventually he understands that it is Ananda, bliss, that is the secret behind and through all existence. The Yoga of devotion focuses directly on the Ananda of union, and thus, can lead the seeker to a status of union at the highest levels. Sri Aurobindo notes: "...yet is delight the nature of consciousness and of the acme of delight love is the key and the secret."

As with Knowledge, so also the Will expressed in works. "And if will is the power of conscious being by which it fulfils itself and by union in will we become one with the Being in its characteristic infinite power, yet all the works of that power start from delight, live in the delight, have delight for their aim and end; love of the Being in itself and in all of itself that its power of consciousness manifests, is the way to the perfect wideness of the Ananda. Love is the power and passion of the divine self-delight and without love we may get the rapt peace of its infinity, the absorbed silence of the Ananda, but not its absolute depth of richness and fullness. Love leads us from the suffering of division into the bliss of perfect union, but without losing that joy of the act of union which is the soul's greatest discovery and for which the life of the cosmos is a long preparation. Therefore to approach God by love is to prepare oneself for the greatest possible spiritual fulfilment."

"Love fulfilled does not exclude knowledge, but itself brings knowledge; and the completer the knowledge, the richer the possibility of love." There is a danger in raising up the passion inherent in love, without bringing the knowledge to play as well. This can lead to fanaticism or narrow formulations of expression. It can be coloured by vital desires and emotions if knowledge is not brought to play in the devotional life. "…but love leading to perfect knowledge brings the infinite and absolute union. Such love is not inconsistent with, but rather throws itself with joy into divine works; for it loves God and is one with him in all his being, and therefore in all beings, and to work for the world is then to feel and fulfil multitudinously one's love for God.

This is the trinity of our powers, the union of all three in God to which we arrive when we start on our journey by the path of devotion, with Love for the Angel of the Way to find in the ecstasy of the divine delight of the All-Lover's being the fulfilment of ours, its secure home and blissful abiding-place and the centre of its universal radiation."

Sri Aurobindo, The Synthesis of Yoga, Part Three: The Yoga of Divine Love, Chapter 1, Love and the Triple Path, pp. 522-523

The Paths of Knowledge and of Devotion Are Equally Capable of Leading to Realisation

It is a somewhat natural tendency in the human mind to treat one's own chosen practice, belief, faith, or mode of development as being superior and other ways as being inferior in nature. The devotee will, in such cases, believe that those who follow the path of Knowledge have simply not understood the direct and fast path to God-realization. Similarly, those who practice the Yoga of Knowledge will frequently look down upon the devotee as representing a simpler, and even imperfect, mode of development. Each path, however, starts from some leading principle within the human instrument, and thus, each one has the power to bring about realization and, in that realization, there is a reconciliation between their differences. No matter what the starting point, and what the mode of development, true spiritual effort will lead to realization.

Sri Aurobindo observes: "Since then in the union of these three powers lies our base of perfection, the seeker of an integral self-fulfilment in the Divine must avoid or throw away, if he has them at all, the misunderstanding and mutual depreciation which we often find existent between the followers of the three paths."

"When the devotee has grasped the power that shall raise him, has really laid hold on love, that in the end purifies and enlarges him as effectively as knowledge can; they are equal powers, though their methods of arriving at the same goal are different."

"The intellect is not in every way superior to the heart; if it opens more readily doors at which the heart is apt to fumble in vain, it is, itself, apt to miss truths which to the heart are very near and easy to hold. And if when the way of thought deepens into spiritual experience, it arrives readily at the ethereal heights, pinnacles, skyey widenesses, it cannot without the aid of the heart fathom the intense and rich abysses and oceanic depths of the divine being and the divine Ananda."

Sri Aurobindo, The Synthesis of Yoga, Part Three: The Yoga of Divine Love, Chapter 1, Love and the Triple Path, pp. 523-524

The Heart Can Be Wiser Than the Mind

Oftentimes practitioners of the Yoga of knowledge will dismiss the value of the practices undertaken by devotees because they are based on an inherent "duality", a separation between the devotee and the object of devotion. The Yoga of Knowledge recognizes the inherent Oneness of all existence, and thus, this duality is considered to be "lesser wisdom".

Sri Aurobindo observes in this regard, however, that the way of devotion has a progressive development: "But worship is only the first step on the path of devotion. Where external worship changes into the inner adoration, real Bhakti begins; that deepens into the intensity of divine love; that love leads to the joy of closeness in our relations with the Divine; the joy of closeness passes into the bliss of union. Love too as well as knowledge brings us to a highest oneness and it gives to that oneness its greatest possible depth and intensity. It is true that love returns gladly upon a difference in oneness, by which the oneness itself becomes richer and sweeter. But here we may say that the heart is wiser than the thought, at least than that thought which fixes upon opposite ideas of the Divine and concentrates on one to the exclusion of the other which seems its contrary; but is really its complement and a means of its greatest fulfilment. This is the weakness of the mind that it limits itself by its thoughts, its positive and negative ideas, the aspects of the Divine Reality that it sees, and tends too much to pit one against the other."

The ultimate forms of knowledge recognize that the Impersonal and the Personal are both aspects of the same "omnipresent Reality", and that "One without a second" is complemented by "All this is the Brahman." The heart of devotion achieves this realization through a relationship with the Personal aspect of the Divine, and the recognition that the entire creation is a manifestation of the Divine, thus making the apparent differences and separations a mechanism for the play of the Divine Ananda.

Sri Aurobindo, The Synthesis of Yoga, Part Three: The Yoga of Divine Love, Chapter 1, Love and the Triple Path, pp. 524-525

Knowledge and Devotion Each Lead to Unity With the Supreme

The mental framework from which the human individual starts the spiritual question has inherent limitations because of the natural tendency of the mind to erect separations, divisions and distinctions and then treat them as if they are real and essential differences. Thus, the seekers on the path of Knowledge frequently focus on the impersonal and absolute Brahman as the sole or at least the highest Truth, and they treat the manifested universe as some form of distraction, dream or illusion of Maya. They seek the Impersonal by abandoning the Personal.

Sri Aurobindo reminds us that this represents an artificial distinction and that the Supreme manifests both in the Impersonal and the Personal, and in the Unmanifest as also in the Manifest.

"But the Divine is beyond our oppositions of ideas, beyond the logical contradictions we make between his aspects. He is not, as we have seen, bound and restricted by exclusive unity; his oneness realizes itself in infinite variation and to the joy of that love has the completest key, without therefore missing the joy of the unity. The highest knowledge and highest spiritual experience by knowledge find his oneness as perfect in his various relations with the Many as in his self-absorbed delight. If to thought the Impersonal seems the wider and higher truth, the Personal a narrower experience, the spirit finds both of them to be aspects of a Reality which figures itself in both, and if there is a knowledge of that Reality to which thought arrives by insistence on the infinite Impersonality, there is also a knowledge of it to which love arrives by insistence on the infinite Personality. The spiritual experience of each leads, if followed to the end, to the same ultimate Truth. By Bhakti as by knowledge, as the Gita tells us, we arrive at unity with the Purushottama, the Supreme who contains in himself the impersonal and numberless personalities, the qualityless and infinite qualities, pure being, consciousness and delight and the endless play of their relations."

Sri Aurobindo, The Synthesis of Yoga, Part Three: The Yoga of Divine Love, Chapter 1, Love and the Triple Path, pp. 525-526

Love Is Fulfilled and Perfected by Knowledge of the Divine

The devotee is not satisfied with the austere and dry path of Knowledge. For a considerable time, the path of Knowledge relies on the processes of the human intellect and there can be a tendency towards intellectualism and philosophy that does not bring with it the spiritual fulfilment. Only when the mental process is overpassed can the path of Knowledge bring the fullness of realization. For the devotee, this is a hard and bitter way. The devotee wants to move directly to the experience of the Divine through the seeking of the heart and the rapture of the union.

Yet, devotion also has its limitations. Sri Aurobindo observes: "On the other hand, love itself is not complete without knowledge. The Gita distinguishes between three initial kinds of Bhakti, that which seeks refuge in the Divine from the sorrows of the world..., that which, desiring, approaches the Divine as the giver of its good,..., and that which attracted by what it already loves , but does not yet know, yearns to know this divine Unknown...; but it gives the palm to the Bhakti that knows. Evidently the intensity of passion which says, 'I do not understand, I love' and, loving, cares not to understand, is not love's last self-expression, but its first, nor is it its highest intensity. Rather as knowledge of the Divine grows, delight in the Divine and love of it must increase. Nor can mere rapture be secure without the foundation of knowledge; to live in what we love, gives that security, and to live in it means to be one with it in consciousness, and oneness of consciousness is the perfect condition of knowledge. Knowledge of the Divine gives to love of the Divine its firmest security, opens to it its own widest joy of experience, raises it to its highest pinnacles of outlook."

Sri Aurobindo, The Synthesis of Yoga, Part Three: The Yoga of Divine Love, Chapter 1, Love and the Triple Path, pg. 526

The Integral Way of Yoga Reconciles the Paths of Knowledge, Love and Works

Just as there is a tendency in the exclusive focus on Knowledge to denigrate the path of Devotion, or for the devotee to look down upon the way of Knowledge, both of these tend to look up Works in the world as something lower, distracting and ultimately something to be avoided as it will interfere with their higher seeking. This view however is partial and founded on the initial misconception that arises when the practitioner identifies so closely with his own path or practice that he fails to recognize that each path finds its way eventually to the Divine, and that none of them are complete without the others.

Sri Aurobindo clarifies the question: "But works are only thus outward and distracting when we have not found oneness of will and consciousness with the Supreme. When once that is found, works become the very power of knowledge and the very outpouring of love. If knowledge is the very state of oneness and love its bliss, divine works are the living power of its light and sweetness."

"But still the widest love fulfilled in knowledge sees the world not as something other and hostile to this joy, but as the being of the Beloved and all creatures as his being, and in that vision divine works find their joy and their justification."

However one starts on the path, the integral seeker eventually will find that all of these powers must support one another and manifest as aspects of one complete identification with the Divine:

"It may commence with the way of love, as with the way of knowledge or of works; but where they meet, is the beginning of its joy of fulfilment. Love it cannot miss, even if it does not start from it; for love is the crown of works and the flowering of knowledge."

Sri Aurobindo, The Synthesis of Yoga, Part Three: The Yoga of Divine Love, Chapter 1, Love and the Triple Path, pp. 526-527

Chapter Two

The Motives of Devotion

The Underlying Basis for the Yoga Of Devotion

For most people the idea of worship is associated with a religious tradition which treats the individual as separate and the object of worship (some form of Divinity) as superior, distant and nevertheless "relateable". The idea is that worship establishes a communication link between the human being and the Divine, and, on the one side, the human being undertakes to worship, and on the other, God rains down his blessings and takes personal interest in the welfare of the worshipping individuals.

For the practitioner of the Yoga of devotion, worship may start out as something akin to the

religious concept, but as the practice deepens, the individual finds that the merging of consciousness into Oneness with the original object of devotion begins to occur, and at some point, the separation and difference actually disappears.

Sri Aurobindo clarifies this: "Yoga in its culmination abolishes the gulf; for Yoga is union. We arrive at union with it through knowledge; for as our first obscure conceptions of it clarify, enlarge, deepen, we come to recognise it as our own highest self, the origin and sustainer of our being and that towards which it tends. We arrive at union with it through works; for from simply obeying we come to identify our will with its Will, since only in proportion as it is identified with this Power that is its source and ideal, can our will become perfect and divine. We arrive at union with it also by worship; for the thought and act of a distant worship develops into the necessity of close adoration and this into the intimacy of love, and the consummation of love is union with the Beloved. it is from this development of worship that the Yoga of devotion starts and it is by this union with the Beloved that it finds its highest point and consummation."

Sri Aurobindo, The Synthesis of Yoga, Part Three: The Yoga of Divine Love, Chapter 2, The Motives of Devotion, pg. 528

The Transformation of Religious Worship Into Pure Bhakti

All human development starts from the basis of the ordinary human nature and its basic capacities, and evolves from there over time through persistent action, attention and dedicated effort. The ego, as the foundation of the human experience, provides the initial impetus and motives for undertaking the process of worship. We seek for some satisfying result, some boon, some support in adversity, or some type of salvation, either now or hereafter.

As the process develops, however, the act of worship begins to separate itself from specific results to be achieved in a personal or egoistic sense and the worship itself becomes its own "goal". Eventually, even this attachment to the experience of worship gives way to something that fills the being and unifies it with the object of devotion, and widens and universalizes the experience of worship. This becomes then the true nature of pure Bhakti.

Sri Aurobindo elaborates this process: "In the transformation of ordinary religious worship into the Yoga of pure Bhakti we see this development from the motived and interested worship of popular religion into a principle of motiveless and self-existent love. This last is in ac the touchstone of the real Bhakti and shows whether we are really in the central way or are only upon one of the bypaths leading to it. We have to throw away the props of our weakness, the motives of the ego, the lures of our lower nature before we can deserve the divine union."

Sri Aurobindo, The Synthesis of Yoga, Part Three: The Yoga of Divine Love, Chapter 2, The Motives of Devotion, pp. 528-529

Fear and Desire Act As Motive Springs of the Evolution of Religion

Sri Aurobindo provides an insightful overview of the development of the religious impulse in humanity. "Faced with the sense of a Power or perhaps a number of Powers greater and higher than himself by whom his life in Nature is overshadowed, influenced, governed, man naturally applies to it or to them the first primitive feelings of the natural being among difficulties, desires and dangers of that life,–fear and interest. The enormous part played by these motives in the evolution of the religious instinct is undeniable, and in fact, man being what he is, it could hardly have been less; and even when religion has advanced fairly far on its road, we see these motives still surviving, active, playing a sufficiently large part, justified and appealed to by Religion herself in support of her claims of man."

When the human being is beset by and overwhelmed by forces of Nature and huge movements of energy both in the physical world and even in human society, the first impulse is to reach out to those forces, personify them and try to propitiate them to save, protect and support one in the face of impending disaster. But religious impulse does not subsist on the energy of fear alone. Desire also plays a part, and humanity then prays to God or Gods (in whatever form they may take depending on the various religious traditions) to provide for one's well-being, satisfy one's desires, or provide a path for salvation in some future heaven or in the next lifetime!

As the individual begins to reflect on how things happen, and begins to recognize that there are Powers at work that move the events that mark his life-experience, he tries to get into contact with those Powers: "As soon, then, as he comes to sense a Power behind all this which can influence or determine action and result, he conceives of it as a dispenser of boons and sufferings, able and under certain conditions willing to help him or hurt, save and destroy."

For much of humanity, these represent the underlying motive springs behind the practice of religion. Some of this is done with direct appeals for specific results, but some is couched in broader terms and higher ideals, yet nevertheless still founded on the vital impulses of fear and desire that are the characteristic of the vital being of man.

Sri Aurobindo, The Synthesis of Yoga, Part Three: The Yoga of Divine Love, Chapter 2, The Motives of Devotion, pp. 529-530

God Seen In the Image of Man

Religious scriptures, particularly in the Judeo-Christian tradition, see man shaped and created in the "image of God". Yet, when we look at the way people tend to view or imagine the God (or Gods) they worship, we see a clear tendency to have God take on human motives and tendencies, and react in particularly human ways.

The Gods of ancient Greece had favorites, carried on love affairs, fought wars and expressed anger, jealousy and hatred on a regular basis. Of course, they also had occasion to express their positive powers of intelligence, beneficence and a sense of justice in their dealings.

God in the Old Testament encouraged and supported his "chosen people" to fight wars and destroy people and societies that worshipped other Gods. The history of Christianity is riddled with instances of God being called upon to defend the faithful and destroy the "heretics" or "heathens", and a victory in warfare was seen as a validation of God's Will and the justness of the cause.

This anthropomorphic view of God is not limited to the religions of the West; rather it is a general human tendency to externalize God and give God human qualities and make him approachable.

When people view God in this light, they believe that through prayer, praise and worship they can influence God to intervene on their part. Sri Aurobindo explains: "…worship is then a means of propitiation by gifts and a supplication by prayer. He gets God on his side by praying to him and flattering him. With a more advanced mentality, he conceives of the action of life as reposing on a certain principle of divine justice, which he reads always according to his own ideas and character, as a sort of enlarged copy of his human justice; he conceives the idea of moral good and evil and looks upon suffering and calamity and all things unpleasant as a punishment for his sins and upon happiness and good fortune and all things pleasant as a reward of his virtue. God appears to him as a king, judge, legislator, executor of justice. But still regarding him as a sort of magnified Man, he imagines that as his own justice can be deflected by prayers and propitiation, so the divine justice can also be deflected by the same means. Justice is to him reward and punishment, and the justice of punishment can be modified by mercy to the suppliant, while rewards can be supplemented by special favours and kindness such as Power when pleased can always bestow on its adherents and worshippers. Moreover God like ourselves is capable of wrath and revenge, and wrath and revenge can be turned by gifts and supplication and atonement; he is capable too of partiality, and his partiality can be attracted by gifts, by prayer and by praise. Therefore instead of relying solely on the observation of the moral law, worship as prayer and propitiation is still continued."

This represents early stages in the evolution of devotion and as the process continues, another understanding begins to replace or at least refine this view.

Sri Aurobindo, The Synthesis of Yoga, Part Three: The Yoga of Divine Love, Chapter 2, The Motives of Devotion, pg. 530

Motives Underlying Popular Religion

Several additional experiences enter into the development of religion. In addition to the fulfillment of desire and the abatement of fear, there may arise a sense of awe at the power and immensity of the creation and natural phenomena. This is a quite natural sense which arises within when one experiences the power of thunder and lightning, the force of the sea, the majesty of mountains, or when one sees the vast diversity and beauty of all the creatures that inhabit the world and their interdependence upon one another in an integrated whole. With this feeling of awe there also naturally arises a sense of veneration, a profound experience of appreciation for the Power that creates all of this, and the Power that manifests in all of this.

Sri Aurobindo observes: "For, even while preserving largely the idea of a God endowed with the qualities of human nature, there still grows up along with it, mixed up with it or superadded, the conception of an omniscience and omnipotence and a mysterious perfection quite other than our nature. A confused mixture of all these motives, variously developed, often modified, subtilised or glossed over, is what constitutes nine-tenths of popular religion; the other tenth is a suffusion of the rest by the percolation into it of nobler, more beautiful and profounder ideas of the Divine which minds of a greater spirituality have been able to bring into the more primitive religious concepts of mankind. The result is usually crude enough and a ready target for the shafts of skepticism and unbelief,–powers of the human mind which have their utility even for faith and religion, since they compel a religion to purify gradually what is crude or false in its conceptions."

For the yogic path of love and devotion, it becomes necessary to understand and extract those conceptions, motives and experiences which are true and which lead to the oneness of spiritual realization from those which are projections of the normal human motivations, externalized into the forms of religious worship.

"for we seek by Bhakti union with the Divine and true relation with it, with its truth and not with any mirage of our lower nature and of its egoistic impulses and ignorant conceptions."

Sri Aurobindo, The Synthesis of Yoga, Part Three: The Yoga of Divine Love, Chapter 2, The Motives of Devotion, pp. 530-531

Experiencing a Conscient Higher Power in the Universe

Sceptics of religion argue that there is no higher Power of creation, whether called God or by any other name, and that the universe manifests out of physical matter and the human intellect is, essentially, the highest manifestation at this time. Others argue that while there may have been a Creator at one point in time, that creator has either died or does not pay attention to the creation, and thus, there is no higher power that intervenes in our lives, thus denying the efficacy of prayer or worship.

One of the major differences between religious faith and Yoga, is that Yoga is a science that bases itself on experience. Sri Aurobindo indicates: "Yoga is not a matter of theory or dogma, like philosophy or popular religion, but a matter of experience."

The seeker practicing Yoga is thus able to experience states of conscious awareness that reveal the higher, universal conscient Presence that is posited in religion and denied by the sceptics: "Its experience is that of a conscient universal and supracosmic Being with whom it brings us into union with the Invisible, always renewable and verifiable, is as valid as our conscious experience of a physical world and of visible bodies with whose invisible minds we daily communicate."

When on reflects deeply on the issue, one can see that the universal creation evolves higher and higher forms of consciousness. This could not evolve if it were not present in an involved form to begin with, just as the oak tree cannot develop from the acorn if it were not involved therein. Similarly, one can see the interdependent structure of the universe as evidence of intelligence. As human intelligence has focused on the structure of existence, we have become aware of forces that were previously "invisible" to us, to the extent that now we can make use of electricity, solar power, wireless communications and microwaves in our daily lives without being able to visibly "see" them. The Yogin understands that there are limitations to the ranges of experience that the mentality can experience in its normal status today; yet that does not limit the opportunity to exceed these limits or for humanity to evolve to new stages of evolutionary development wherein further realms of experience are made manifest.

Sri Aurobindo observes: "Yoga proceeds by conscious union, the conscious being is its instrument, and a conscious union with the Inconscient cannot be. It is true that it goes beyond the human consciousness and in Samadhi becomes superconscient, but this is not an annullation of our conscious being, it is only its self-exceeding, the going beyond its present level and normal limits."

Sri Aurobindo, The Synthesis of Yoga, Part Three: The Yoga of Divine Love, Chapter 2, The Motives of Devotion, pp. 531-532

Considering the Underlying Question of the Personality of the Divine

The basis of the Yoga of knowledge is the Impersonality of the Divine. The basis of the Yoga of devotion, however, is the Personality of the Divine. Religion, as we have seen, creates a relationship between human and the Divine; through prayer, adoration and emotional submission the human elicits a response from this Divine Personality. The Yoga of devotion also focuses on the Divine Personality and develops an intimate and personal relationship to this Divine Being. For the practitioner following the path of devotion, the divine Impersonality is only one aspect, and not the sole aspect of creation. The reality and effectivity of the Yoga of devotion depends on the reality and existence of a Divine Being capable of relation with the individual in a personal way.

Sri Aurobindo observes: "In both [religion and the Yoga of Bhakti] the human being approaches the Divine by means of his humanity, with human emotions as he would approach a fellow being, but with more intense and exalted feelings; and not only so, but the Divine also responds in a manner answering to these emotions. In that possibility of response lies the whole question; for if the Divine is impersonal, featureless and relationless, no such response is possible and all human approach to it becomes an absurdity; we must rather dehumanise, depersonalise, annual ourselves in so far as we are human beings or any kind of beings; on no other conditions and by no other means can we approach it. Love, fear, prayer, praise, worship of an Impersonality which has no relation with us or with anything in the universe and no feature that our minds can lay hold of, are obviously an irrational foolishness. On such terms religion and devotion become out of the question."

Sri Aurobindo, The Synthesis of Yoga, Part Three: The Yoga of Divine Love, Chapter 2, The Motives of Devotion, pg. 532

The Yoga of Devotion Seeks a Divine Fulfillment Through Personal Relations with the Divine

The Yoga of devotion takes up the basic nature of the human being and both acknowledges and accepts the idea that the part of our being that is capable of emotion, relationship, love and devotion actually has its rationale and basis and that we can approach the Divine from this inherent aspect of our nature.

The path of devotion does not accept the finality or sole existence of the Impersonal Divine without a personal aspect. Sri Aurobindo explains: "We can obey it as a Law, lift our souls to it in aspiration towards its tranquil being, grow into it by shedding from us our emotional nature; the human being in us is not satisfied, but is quieted, balanced, stilled."

This highlights the essential difference in approach between the Yoga of knowledge and the Yoga of devotion: "But the Yoga of devotion, agreeing in this with Religion, insists on a closer and warmer worship than this impersonal aspiration. It aims at a divine fulfilment of the humanity in us as well as of the impersonal part of our being; it aims at a divine satisfaction of the emotional being of man. It demands of the Supreme acceptance of our love and a response in kind; as we delight in Him and seek Him, so it believes that He too delights in us and seeks us."

In response to the idea that it is irrational to assume that the Divine either can or does take notice in the human individual, the Yoga of devotion holds that it is this Divine notice that creates the possibility for the human turning towards the Divine in the first place: "...for if the supreme and universal Being did not take any delight in us, it is not easy to see how we could have come into being or could remain in being, and if He does not at all draw us towards him,–a divine seeking of us,–there would seem to be no reason in Nature why we should turn from the round of our normal existence to seek Him."

Sri Aurobindo, The Synthesis of Yoga, Part Three: The Yoga of Divine Love, Chapter 2, The Motives of Devotion, pp. 532-533

The Yoga of Devotion Needs for Four Basic Principles to Be True

For those who hold that the universe is some mechanism without a creator, or a machinery that does not have any direct relationship with the creator who "abandoned" it after creation, there can be no justification for a Yoga based on devotion. For those who believe the only reality is the Absolute, unmoving, silent and uninvolved in the play of the outer life, which they term illusion or Maya, again, there can be no Yoga of devotion.

In order to have a Yoga of devotion that can actually achieve a true realization of the Divine, Sri Aurobindo has identified four basic principles: "Therefore, that there may be at all any possibility of a Yoga of devotion, we must admit first that the supreme Existence is not an abstraction or a state of existence, but a conscious Being; secondly, that he meets us in the universe and is in some way immanent in it as well as its source,–otherwise, we should have to go out of cosmic life to meet him; thirdly, that he is capable of personal relations with us and must therefore not be incapable of personality; finally, that when we approach him by our human emotions, we receive a response in kind."

Sri Aurobindo goes on to clarify these points: "This does not mean that the nature of the Divine is precisely the same as our human nature though upon a larger scale, or that it is that nature pure of certain perversions and God a magnified or else an ideal Man. God is not and cannot be an ego limited by his qualities as we are in our normal consciousness."

There must be a correspondence between the human and the divine consciousness, or else they could not communicate with one another. To be sure, the human consciousness may be limited in its range and capacities, but it still must adhere to essential principles that bring it into contact with and able to interact with the divine consciousness. "…still our human emotions and impulses must have behind them a Truth in him of which they are the limited and very often, therefore, the perverse or even the degraded forms. By approaching him through our emotional being we approach that Truth, it comes down to us to meet our emotions and lift them towards it; through it our emotional being is united with him."

Sri Aurobindo, The Synthesis of Yoga, Part Three: The Yoga of Divine Love, Chapter 2, The Motives of Devotion, pp. 533-534

The Divine Accepts and Responds to the Seeker Commensurate to the Seeking

Since the seeker of the Divine necessarily begins with the foundation of his human consciousness, the initial forms and methods of the seeking, whether through knowledge, works or devotion, will necessarily be limited and distorted from the reality. As the relationship grows and the seeker thereby refines his understanding, the mode of the seeking and the understand get refined and approach closer to the truth. The Bhagavad Gita advises us that in whatever way a seeker worships the Divine, the Divine acknowledges.

Sri Aurobindo summarizes: "Even as men approach him, so he accepts them and responds too by the divine Love to their Bhakti…. Whatever form of being, whatever qualities they lend him, through that form and those qualities he helps them to develop, encourages or governs their advance and in their straight way or their crooked draws them towards him. What they see of him is a truth, but a truth represented to them in the terms of their own being and consciousness, partially, distortedly, not in the terms of its own higher reality, not in the aspect which it assumes when we become aware of the complete Divinity."

The various religious forms of worship are an entrance gate, and thus, have their own rationale. "They are justified because there is a truth of the Divine behind them and only so could that truth of the Divine be approached in that stage of the developing human consciousness and be helped forward; they are condemned, because to persist always in these crude conceptions and relations with the Divine is to miss that closer union towards which these crude beginnings are the first steps, however faltering."

Sri Aurobindo, The Synthesis of Yoga, Part Three: The Yoga of Divine Love, Chapter 2, The Motives of Devotion, pg. 534

Love Is the Key to Achievement of the Self-Existent Delight of Existence

The evolutionary unfolding of consciousness in Nature develops from a state of unconsciousness to an ever-increasing focus and attempt to achieve union with the Divine. At the stage of development represented by humanity, this seeking can become conscious, as the individual begins to understand the drive towards unity, and from that point forward, focused efforts can be made to turn the being more and more towards the Divine through worship, adoration, devotion and love. The development of religion is an early attempt to harness this drive and focus it.

The Yoga of devotion begins when the seeker goes beyond the limitations that tie themselves to specific forms, rituals or methodologies, and begins to grasp the larger goal. Sri Aurobindo describes it thus: "But it does not become what we specifically call Yoga until the motive becomes in a certain degree clairvoyant, until it sees that union is its object and that love is the principle of union, and until therefore it tries to realise love and lose its separative character in love."

"Thus the motives of devotion have first to direct themselves engrossingly and predominantly towards the Divine, then to transform themselves so that they are rid of their more earthy elements and finally to take their stand in pure and perfect love. All those that cannot coexist with the perfect union of love, must eventually fall away, while only those that can form themselves into expressions of divine love and into means of enjoying divine love, can remain. For love is the one emotion in us which can be entirely motiveless and self-existent; love need have no other motive than love. For all our emotions arise either from the seeking after delight and the possession of it, or from the baffling of the search, or from the failure of the delight we have possessed or had thought to grasp; but love is that by which we can enter directly into possession of the self-existent delight of the divine Being. Divine love is indeed itself that possession and, as it were, the body of the Ananda."

Sri Aurobindo, The Synthesis of Yoga, Part Three: The Yoga of Divine Love, Chapter 2, The Motives of Devotion, pp. 534-535

Love Is the Ultimate Motive of Devotion

The mind of man looks at the devotional nature and is able to raise numerous questions which are unable to be precisely answered to the satisfaction of the intellect. The Yoga of love and devotion is a matter for the heart, not the mind, and the truth that is understood by the seeker in this path is one that satisfies the deeper sense that transcends the mental formulations. The mind is necessarily limited by its framework based in division, separation and exclusion, and its need to analyze; while the heart is able to heal division, breach separation, include all and join things together. It is this difference in capacity and way of knowledge that precludes the intellect standing in judgment over the heart's seeking and finding.

This implies, as Sri Aurobindo relates: "The truth of the motives of the heart's devotion and their final arrival and in some sort their disappearance into the supreme and unique self-existent motive of love is therefore all that initially and essentially concerns us." He indicates that all the questions about specific forms that the Divine may take, and specific ways that the individual can interface and relate to the Divine are not essential for the heart that takes up this path and devotes itself to the way of love.

"…all we need at present say is that the Divine does at least accept the various forms which the devotee gives to him and through them meets him in love, while the mixing of our spirits with his spirit is essential to the fruition of Bhakti."

There are those who argue that there must be an eternal difference between God and the devotee for devotion to be able to take place; while there are those who argue that all such differences are part of the illusion presented by the lesser reality of the outer world. Neither of these positions need interfere with the truth experienced by the devotee through the heart's devotion. "We may hold, however, the truth of the one existence in this sense that all in Nature is the Divine even though God may be more than all in Nature, and love becomes then a movement by which the Divine in Nature and man takes possession of and enjoys the delight of the universal and the supreme Divine. In any case, love has necessarily a twofold fulfilment by its very nature, that by which the lover and the beloved enjoy their union in difference and all too that enhances the joy of various union, and that by which they throw themselves into each other and become one Self. That truth is quite sufficient to start with, for it is the very nature of love, and since love is the essential motive of this Yoga, as is the whole nature of love, so will be too the crown and fulfilment of the movement of the Yoga."

Sri Aurobindo, The Synthesis of Yoga, Part Three: The Yoga of Divine Love, Chapter 2, The Motives of Devotion, pp. 535-536

CHAPTER THREE

THE GODWARD EMOTIONS

The Main Principle of the Yoga of Love and Devotion

Each path of Yoga focuses on an aspect or power of the being, which it then works to transform and refocus on the Divine. While the path of works, focuses on the power of the will in action, and the path of knowledge focuses on the intelligent reasoning power of the mind, the path of devotion aims to turn the focus and intensify the action of the emotional powers of the being.

Just as each path utilizes a different capability of the human being, so each one focuses its effort on attainment of a different aspect of the Divine. The Yoga of knowledge will seek the stillness, peace and infinite awareness of the Divine consciousness; the Yoga of works will seek the transformation of all action into an expression of the Divine Will; and the Yoga of devotion seeks to bring about the joy or bliss of union with the Divine Presence.

Sri Aurobindo describes the Yoga of devotion thus: "Its main principle is to adopt some human relation between man and the Divine Being by which through the ever intenser flowing of the heart's emotions towards him the human soul may at last be wedded to and grow one with him in a passion of divine Love."

The emotional nature is fully engaged: "Every feeling that can make the heart ready for this ecstasy the Yoga admits; everything that detracts from it must increasingly drop away as the strong union of love becomes closer and more perfect."

Sri Aurobindo, The Synthesis of Yoga, Part Three: The Yoga of Divine Love, Chapter 3, The Godward Emotions, pg. 537

The Fear of God and the Yoga of Devotion

One of the earliest motives that lead to religious worship of the Divine is that of fear. The power and majesty of God are on display through the works of Nature and the human individual, small, weak, limited and subject to control by those larger forces, frequently approaches these powers of God with a sense of awe or fear. In a more developed religion there arises an institutional form of modulating this response through creation of sets of rules or principles of action; the failure to adhere to this codified series of rules of conduct leads to divine retribution or divine justice being meted out to the individual who has transgressed.

Sri Aurobindo observes: "In certain religions, in most perhaps, the idea of the fear of God plays a very large part, sometimes the largest, and the God-fearing man is the typical worshiper of these religions. The sentiment of fear is indeed perfectly consistent with devotion of a certain kind and up to a certain point; at its highest it rises into a worship of the divine Power, the divine Justice, divine Law, divine Righteousness, and ethical obedience, an awed reverence for the almighty Creator and Judge.... It regards God as the King and does not approach too near the glory of his throne unless justified by righteousness or led there by a mediator who will turn away the divine wrath for sin. Even when it draws nearest, it keeps an awed distance between itself and the high object of its worship. It cannot embrace the Divine with all the fearless confidence of the child in his mother or of the lover in his beloved or with that intimate sense of oneness which perfect love brings with it."

The Yoga of devotion aims to bridge the gap between the Divine and the human through establishing the unity or Oneness between them; thus, eventually the sense of distinction or separation that underlies the fear of God must be overcome for the perfection of this yogic path.

Sri Aurobindo, The Synthesis of Yoga, Part Three: The Yoga of Divine Love, Chapter 3, The Godward Emotions, pp. 537-538

The Root and Origin of Divine Fear

An individual born into the world experiences innumerable forces which can harm or kill him. Some of them are awe-inspiring in their intensity. The tornado or the typhoon, the earthquake or the volcano are just a few of the powers of Nature that bring an inner recognition that there are things that are more powerful than can be comprehended, and which are impossible for the individual to control. The ocean, the mountains, the intensity of the sun also provide an overwhelming experience of smallness and weakness in the individual's being. Other powers of Nature, including other beings in the world, as well as the changes brought about by weather and season, reinforce the sense that there are powers that are larger, stronger and dominating which act upon us and do their will with us.

The simple natural man could simply react in awe. As humanity developed, and codes of social and moral conduct were developed, a natural evolution took place to begin to attribute the actions of these forces to a capacity to judge and exact retribution on the individual. The ancient Greeks developed a keen sense of how certain attitudes would bring forth the powers that pulled the overly proud down from their heights and humbled them. Other cultures developed similar forms of understanding.

Sri Aurobindo observes: "It was the perception of powers in the world greater than man, obscure in their nature and workings, which seemed always ready to strike him down in his prosperity and to smite him for any actions which displeased them."

As mankind began to delve deeply into the operations of Nature, some began to assert that the actions that had elicited fear of divine justice or retribution were actually the natural operation of nature unconnected to any individual's specific mode of conduct. Yet the basis of the sense of divine intervention remains at the core of a number of major religious traditions.

"Fear of the gods arose from man's ignorance of God and his ignorance of the laws that govern the world. It attributed to the higher powers caprice and human passion; it made them in the image of the great ones of the earth, capable of whim, tyranny, personal enmity, jealous of any greatness in man which might raise him above the littleness of terrestrial nature and bring him too near to the divine nature."

The idea that the gods required propitiation, adoration, and worship and that by undertaking such acts, they would support and uphold the individual and provide prosperity and beneficence and keep the individual from harm, corresponded to the ways human beings interacted in their societies and governmental management structures.

"With such notions no real devotion could arise, except that doubtful kind which the weaker may feel for the stronger whose protection he can buy by worship and gifts and propitiation and obedience to such laws as he may have laid upon those beneath him and may enforce by rewards and punishments, or else the submissive and prostrate reverence and adoration which one may feel for a greatness, glory, wisdom, sovereign power which is above the world and is the source or at any rate the regulator of all its laws and happenings."

Sri Aurobindo, The Synthesis of Yoga, Part Three: The Yoga of Divine Love, Chapter 3, The Godward Emotions, pg. 538

The Idea of a Divine Ruler or Law-Giver Limits the Development of Devotion

As humanity has developed, the view of God has been refined. One of the early refinements beyond the rudimentary reactions of desire and fear as the basis for worship, was the expression of God as a divine king or ruler, who made laws for humanity to live by, and who rewarded those who were faithful to those laws, and punished those who were not. A further refinement came about with the concept of such rewards or punishments coming after death in the form of an eternal repose in heaven or an eternal torment in hell.

Sri Aurobindo comments: "But even apart fro these extravagances of a childish religious belief, the idea of the almighty Judge, Legislator, King, is a crude and imperfect idea of the Divine, when taken by itself, because it takes an inferior and an external truth for the main truth and it tends to prevent a higher approach to a more intimate reality. It exaggerates the importance of the sense of sin and thereby prolongs and increases the soul's fear and self-distrust and weakness. It attaches the pursuit of virtue and the shunning of sin to the idea of rewards and punishment, though given in an after life, and makes them dependent on the lower motives of fear and interest instead of the higher spirit which should govern the ethical being. It makes hell and heaven and not the Divine himself the object of the human soul in its religious living."

The seeker of the Yoga of devotion overpasses this stage by focusing on "...the inner relations of the human soul with the Divine; but it is these which are the proper field of Yoga."

Sri Aurobindo, The Synthesis of Yoga, Part Three: The Yoga of Divine Love, Chapter 3, The Godward Emotions, pp. 538-539

Transitioning From Religion to the Yoga of Devotion

Each religious sentiment can act as a starting point for a transition to the Yoga of love and devotion. Those who may begin with fear of God, and develop a sense of a Divine judge and lawgiver may grow into a broader conception which breaks out of the limitations of a more narrow religious coda and moral judgments based on it.

Sri Aurobindo observes: "First, there can emerge the idea of the Divine as the source and law and aim of our ethical being and from this there can come the knowledge of him as the highest Self to which our active nature aspires, the Will to which we have to assimilate our will, the eternal Right and Purity and Truth and Wisdom into harmony with which our nature has to grow and towards whose being our being is attracted. By this way we arrive at the Yoga of works, and this Yoga has a place for personal devotion to the Divine, for the divine Will appears as the Master of our works to whose voice we must listen, whose divine impulsion we must obey and whose work it is the sole business of our active life and will to do. Secondly, there emerges the idea of the divine Spirit, the father of all who extends his wings of benignant protection and love over all his creatures, and from that grows between the soul and the Divine the relation of father and child, a relation of love, and as a result, the relation of brotherhood with our fellow-beings. These relations of the Divine into the calm pure light of whose nature we have to grow and the Master whom we approach through works and service, the Father who responds to the love of the soul that approaches him as the child, are admitted elements of the Yoga of devotion."

Sri Aurobindo, The Synthesis of Yoga, Part Three: The Yoga of Divine Love, Chapter 3, The Godward Emotions, pp. 539-540

The Transition from Ethical Action to Divine Nature

Fear of God, which includes fear of punishment and fear of eternal damnation, has been seen as a primary motivating driver towards ethical and moral rectitude in the interactions of the individual with others in society. It plays a role in social interactions and in schooling the soul in higher forms of interaction than simply giving in to impulse of desire or reaction of fear in the world. Sri Aurobindo reminds us however: "When we grow into spirituality, this motive can no longer remain except by the lingering on of some confusion in the mind, some persistence of the old mentality."

Yoga does not look at ethical behavior in the same way that religions or social scientists may do so. The goal in Yoga is to prepare the inner psychological makeup of the seeker to unify with the higher and subtler powers of the Divine, and in order for this to take place, the actions based on Tamas and Rajas have to more and more give way to the development of a Sattwic nature. "But to the Yogin action is chiefly important not for its own sake, but rather as a means for the growth of the soul Godward. Therefore what Indian spiritual writings lay stress upon is not so much the quality of the action to be done as the quality of the soul from which the action flows, upon its truth, fearlessness, purity, love, compassion, benevolence, absence of the will to hurt, and upon the actions as their outflowings.

The Indian approach is the opposite of that taken in the Judeo-Christian tradition, which holds human nature as inherently weak, bad or even perverse, such that the practice of ethical actions and the development of virtuous conduct is seen as a difficult discipline punctuated with weakness of the flesh and failures and recriminations with penalties extracted to train the lower being into the right path. "Our nature contains, as well as its passionate rajasic and its downward-tending tamasic quality, a purer sattwic element and it is the encouragement of this, its highest part, which is the business of ethics. By it we increase the divine nature…, which is present in us and get rid of the Titanic and demoniac elements. Not therefore the Hebraic righteousness of the God-fearing man, but the purity, love, beneficence, truth, fearlessness, harmlessness of the saint and the God-lover are the goal of the ethical growth according to this notion. And, speaking more largely, to grow into the divine nature is the consummation of the ethical being.. This can be done best by realizing God as the higher Self, the guiding and uplifting Will or the Master whom we love and serve. Not fear of him, but love of him and aspiration to the freedom and eternal purity of his being must be the motive."

Sri Aurobindo, The Synthesis of Yoga, Part Three: The Yoga of Divine Love, Chapter 3, The Godward Emotions, pp. 540-541

Putting Aside Fear As a Motive in the Relation Between God and Man

The sense of fear in relation to the Divine accompanies the seeker for some time. As long as there is any sense of difference, any sense of superiority the emotion of fear can creep in. Even Arjuna, who was given the vision of the supreme Divine form in the Bhagavad Gita, was overcome with a sense of fear when he realized that the person he joked with and treated in a casual manner was now able to reveal his divine side to him. He begged for forgiveness at that moment. And he prayed that Sri Krishna would treat him as a friend to a friend, a father to a son, a teacher to a disciple, all relations where trust and love ruled the relationship.

As the seeker progresses in the yogic path of Bhakti, however, the sense of fear must inevitably disappear. The relationship must change to one of unconditioned and unconditional love; and in such a relationship fear has no place. Sri Aurobindo discusses this transition: "The Divine even as the Master does not punish anybody, does not threaten, does not force obedience. It is the human soul that has freely to come to the Divine and offer itself to his overpowering force that he may seize and uplift it towards his own divine levels, and give it that joy of mastery of the finite nature by the Infinite and of service to the Highest by which there comes freedom from the ego and the lower nature. Love is the key of this relation, and this service…, is in Indian Yoga the happy service of the divine Friend or the passionate service to the divine Beloved. The Master of the worlds who in the Gita demands of his servant, the Bhakta, to be nothing more in life than his instrument, makes this claim as the friend, the guide, the higher Self, and describes himself as the Lord of all worlds who is the friend of all creatures…; the two relations in fact must go together and neither can be perfect without the other."

"Love is the real key in both, and perfect love is inconsistent with the admission of the motive of fear. Closeness of the human soul to the Divine is the object, and fear sets always a barrier and a distance; even awe and reverence for the divine Power are a sign of distance and division and they disappear in the intimacy of the union of love. Moreover, fear belongs to the lower nature, to the lower self, and in approaching the higher Self must be put aside before we can enter into its presence."

Sri Aurobindo, The Synthesis of Yoga, Part Three: The Yoga of Divine Love, Chapter 3, The Godward Emotions, pp. 541-542

The Basis and Efficacy of Prayer

Prayer is frequently invoked as a means of putting our personal needs or desires before God, so that God can personally respond and answer those prayers. This is in fact a major basis of the religious viewpoint on prayer. This basis is often ridiculed by those who do not accept the idea that there is a personal Judge or Creator God, sitting on a throne in the sky, who listens to and responds individually to prayer.

As long as we look at the situation from the perspective of the human mind, we try to understand prayer from a dualistic viewpoint. Thus, prayer goes up from a separated individual to a separate God who then responds (or not) to the individual putting up the prayer.

Sri Aurobindo takes a somewhat different view of the matter in his explanation as to the basis and true efficacy of prayer. His explanation is based on the inherent unity of all creation and the oneness of the individual soul with the Divine: "It is true that the universal will executes always its aim and cannot be deflected by egoistic propitiation and entreaty, it is true of the Transcendent who expresses himself in the universal order that, being omniscient, his larger knowledge must foresee the thing to be done and it does not need direction or stimulation by human thought and that the individual's desires are not and cannot be in any world-order the true determining factor. But neither is that order or the execution of the universal will altogether effected by mechanical Law, but by powers and forces of which for human life at least, human will, aspiration and faith are not among the least important. Prayer is only a particular form given to that will, aspiration and faith. Its forms are very often crude and not only childlike, which is in itself no defect, but childish; but still it has a real power and significance. Its power and sense is to put the will, aspiration and faith of man into touch with the divine Will as that of a conscious Being with whom we can enter into conscious and living relations. For our will and aspiration can act either by our own strength and endeavour, which can no doubt be made a thing great and effective whether for lower or higher purposes,..., or it can act in dependence upon and with subordination to the divine or the universal Will. And this latter way, again, may either look upon that Will as responsive indeed to our aspiration, but almost mechanically, by a sort of law of energy, or at any rate quite impersonally, or else it may look upon it as responding consciously to the divine aspiration and faith of the human soul and consciously bringing to it the help, the guidance, the protection and fruition demanded...."

Prayer seen in this light represents the action of the Divine Will unfolding itself in the universal manifestation and expressing itself through the individual soul as an expression of that Will.

Sri Aurobindo, The Synthesis of Yoga, Part Three: The Yoga of Divine Love, Chapter 3, The Godward Emotions, pp. 542-543

The Transformation of Prayer Into Conscious Interchange With the Divine Presence

The initial stages of prayer start with an egoistic self-seeking of desire for some benefit to be obtained from God. There is the consciousness of the limited human ego and an awareness of a great Power or Presence, and prayer acts as the medium of contact that is intended to bring about the result sought by the human ego. Yet it is possible to transform prayer into something purer and higher than this initial stage.

Sri Aurobindo observes: "...but afterwards we can draw towards the spiritual truth which is behind it. It is not then the giving of the thing asked for that matters, but the relation itself, the contact of man's life with God, the conscious interchange. In spiritual matters and in the seeking of spiritual gains, this conscious relation is a great power; it is a much greater power than our own entirely self-reliant struggle and effort and it brings a fuller spiritual growth and experience.

Necessarily, in the end prayer either ceases in the greater thing for which it prepared us,–in fact the form we call prayer is not itself essential so long as the faith, the will, the aspiration are there,–or remains only for the joy of the relation. Also its objects, the *artha* or interest it seeks to realise, becomes higher and higher until we reach the highest motiveless devotion, which is that of divine love pure and simple without any other demand or longing."

As we see in the practice of Raja Yoga, that concentration on an object provides knowledge about that object, eventually ending in knowledge by identity; so too in the Yoga of devotion, prayer acts as the process that brings the consciousness of the human seeker into direct contact and relation with the Divine consciousness, and as the process deepens, the truth of Oneness replaces prayer with identity and the bliss of unity.

Sri Aurobindo, The Synthesis of Yoga, Part Three: The Yoga of Divine Love, Chapter 3, The Godward Emotions, pg. 543

Three Types of Devotional Seekers and the Divine Relations They Obtain

In the Bhagavad Gita, Sri Krishna acknowledges that in whatever way a seeker approaches the Divine, he is met by a response. There is no door too small, and no motive too egoistic. The operative factor is the turning of the consciousness, in some way, for whatever ostensible purpose, to the Divine, and thereby to create an interchange and a relationship. Through that relationship the energy flows and over time, this brings about growth and transformative changes for the seeker.

The Gita also describes four broad classes of seekers, based on the initial motive by which they turn to the Divine. Sri Aurobindo describes the first three of these as follows: "The relations which arise out of this attitude towards the Divine, are that of the divine Father and the Mother with the child and that of the divine Friend. To the Divine as these things the human soul comes for help, for protection, for guidance, for fruition,–or if knowledge be the aim, to the Guide, Teacher, Giver of light, for the Divine is the Sun of knowledge,–or it comes in pain and suffering for relief and solace and deliverance, it may be deliverance either from the suffering itself or from all world-existence which is the habitat of the suffering or from all its inner and real causes. (These are three of the four classes of devotees which are recognised by the Gita…, the distressed, the seeker of personal objects and the seeker of God-knowledge.)"

Each of these has a different intensity of relation between the seeker and the Divine. "For the relation of fatherhood is always less close, intense, passionate, intimate, and therefore it is less resorted to in the Yoga which seeks for the closest union. That of the divine friend is a thing sweeter and more intimate, admits of an equality and intimacy even in inequality and the beginning of mutual self-giving; at its closest when all idea of other giving and taking disappears, when this relation becomes motiveless except for the one all-sufficing motive of love, it turns into the free and happy relation of the playmate in the Lila of existence. But closer and more intimate still is the relation of the Mother and the child, and that therefore plays a very large part wherever the religious impulse is most richly fervent and springs most warmly from the heart of man. The soul goes to the Mother-Soul in all its desires and troubles, and the Divine Mother wishes that it should be so, so that she may pour out her heart of love. It turns to her too because of the self-existent nature of this love and because that points us to the home towards which we turn from our wanderings in the world and to the bosom in which we find our rest."

Sri Aurobindo, The Synthesis of Yoga, Part Three: The Yoga of Divine Love, Chapter 3, The Godward Emotions, pp. 543-544

The Passionate Embrace of the Lover and the Beloved in Bhakti Yoga

Bhakti Yoga takes on the various forms of relationships of love and turns them towards the Divine. The most intimate and passionate of these is that of the Lover and the Beloved. The various devotional practices of religion tend to avoid this form due to the potential for it being misdirected toward outer forms in a perversion of the true and inner devotional passion that motivates it. The very power of this form elicits fear in those who follow a less intense path. In its purest form, however, this relationship brings forth the utter surrender of the soul to God, without any motives of desire or any attempt to escape from suffering; rather, the relationship and the intensity of the relationship are the goal unto themselves.

Sri Aurobindo describes it thus: "Wherever there is the desire of the soul for its utter union with God, this form of the divine yearning makes its way even into religions which seem to do without it and give it no place in their ordinary system. Here the one thing asked for is love, the one thing feared is the loss of love, the one sorrow is the sorrow of separation of love; for all other things either do not exist for the lover or come in only as incidents or as results and not as objects or conditions of love."

All the forms of devotion or love of the Divine eventually obtain a response, and to the extent that they start from a desire for relief, or for some worldly motive, they may obtain even those things; but eventually they have to give way to the motiveless devotion. The way of the Lover goes straight to the heart of this issue and dispenses with all desire for outer satisfactions; rather it seeks love pure, constant and eternal.

"But here the beginning is love and the end is love and the whole aim is love. There is indeed the desire of possession, but even this is overcome in the fullness of the self-existent love and the final demand of the Bhakta is simply that his Bhakti may never cease nor diminish. He does not ask for heaven or for liberation from birth or for any other object, but only that his love may be eternal and absolute."

Sri Aurobindo, The Synthesis of Yoga, Part Three: The Yoga of Divine Love, Chapter 3, The Godward Emotions, pp. 544-545

Love Absolute and Eternal

The essence of Bhakti Yoga is love. Human love attempts to develop an intense bond between different individuals as an attempt to bridge the gap of separation. Of all human bonds, the bond of love is the most intense. There are different forms of love, the love of parent for child, the love of friend for friend, but the ultimate experience of human love is that of lover and beloved. Bhakti Yoga turns each form of love towards the divine, including that of the lover and the beloved, and this is the inner secret of the Vaishnava in the ecstatic bliss of the Krishna Lila.

Sri Aurobindo observes: "Passing beyond desire of possession which means a difference, it is a seeking for oneness, and it is here that the idea of oneness, of two souls merging into each other and becoming one finds the acme of its longing and the utterness of its satisfaction. Love, too, is a yearning for beauty, and it is here that the yearning is eternally satisfied in the vision and the touch and the joy of the All-beautiful. Love is a child and a seeker of Delight, and it is here that it finds the highest possible ecstasy both of the heart-consciousness and of every fibre of the being. Moreover, this relation is that which as between human being and human being demands the most and, even while reaching the greatest intensities, is still the least satisfied, because only in the Divine can it find its real and its utter satisfaction. Therefore it is here most that the turning of human emotion Godwards finds its full meaning and discovers all the truth of which love is the human symbol, all its essential instincts divinised, raised, satisfied in the bliss from which our life was born and towards which by oneness it returns in the Ananda of the divine existence where love is absolute, eternal and unalloyed."

Sri Aurobindo, The Synthesis of Yoga, Part Three: The Yoga of Divine Love, Chapter 3, The Godward Emotions, pg. 545

CHAPTER FOUR

THE WAY OF DEVOTION

Four Essential Steps in the Yoga of Devotion

The Yoga of Devotion is based on turning the emotional being towards the Divine. Over many millenia, across the entire gamut of human experience, there have been numerous attempts to systematise practices that will bring about the intense emotional union of human with divine. This has led to a wide range of rituals, prayers or habitual actions that we see in any devotional service or practice. This may include the use of rosaries, regimented times of prayer, or devotional singing or dance. The practices may be done in solitary locations or in large groups.

All of these practices arose and became systematised based on real breakthrough events that people were able to experience, and the attempt to create out of those experiences some kind of reproducible methodology.

Sri Aurobindo observes, in this regard: "Bhakti in itself is as wide as the heart-yearning of the soul for the Divine and as simple and straightforward as love and desire going straight towards their object. It cannot, therefore, be fixed down to any systematic method, cannot found itself on a psychological science like the Rajayoga, or a psycho-physical like the Hathayoga, or start from a definite intellectual process like the ordinary method of the Jnanayoga. It may employ various means or supports, and man, having in him a tendency towards order, process and system, may try to methodise his resort to these auxiliaries: but to give an account of their variations one would have to review almost all man's numberless religions upon their side of inner approach to the Deity."

He proceeds further to break down the four steps or movements that are essential to Bhakti Yoga: "...the desire of the Soul when it turns towards God and the straining of its emotion towards him, the pain of love and the divine return of love, the delight of love possessed and the play of that delight, and the eternal enjoyment of the divine Lover which is the heart of celestial bliss."

By reviewing each of these steps, it will be possible to develop a general guideline both for the practice of Bhakti Yoga and for the incorporation, to the extent they are useful, of the principles of Bhakti into the Integral Yoga.

Sri Aurobindo, The Synthesis of Yoga, Part Three: The Yoga of Divine Love, Chapter 4, The Way of Devotion, pg. 546

Adoration Is the First Phase of the Turning of the Soul to the Divine

For the human individual, as he begins to focus on the Divine, the first stage is generally one of the feeling of adoration. Sri Aurobindo comments: "In ordinary religion this adoration wears the form of external worship and that again develops a most external form of ceremonial worship."

Most individuals find it difficult, particularly in the beginning to focus this emotional force purely internally without any concrete external form for reference; thus, we see the development of rituals, ceremonies and specific forms that are created as objects of worship, to stand in place of the Divine who remains unseen. As long as this adoration and worship has a real force behind it, it can accomplish something real and useful in the development; however, many times these external forms may lose their inner life-energy and become mere rote repetition or habit without a vivifying force.

"It is evident that even real religion,–and Yoga is something more than religion,–only begins when this quite outward worship corresponds to something really felt within the mind, some genuine submission, awe or spiritual aspiration, to which it becomes an aid, an outward expression and also a sort of periodical or constant reminder helping to draw back the mind to it from the preoccupations of ordinary life."

Yoga goes beyond this stage because it does not accept the adoration or worship, which implies separation, division and difference, as an appropriate goal or stopping point; rather, Yoga implies union with the Divine.

"The aim of Yoga being union, its beginning must always be a seeking after the Divine, a longing after some kind of touch, closeness or possession. When this comes on us, the adoration becomes always primarily an inner worship; we begin to make ourselves a temple of the Divine, our thoughts and feelings a constant prayer of aspiration and seeking, our whole life an external service and worship. It is as this change, this new soul-tendency grows, that the religion of the devotee becomes a Yoga, a growing contact and union. It does not follow that the outward worship will necessarily be dispensed with, but it will increasingly become only a physical expression or outflowing of the inner devotion and adoration, the wave of the soul throwing itself out in speech and symbolic act."

Sri Aurobindo, The Synthesis of Yoga, Part Three: The Yoga of Divine Love, Chapter 4, The Way of Devotion, pp. 546-547

Inner Purification and Consecration of the Being

For the practitioner of Bhakti Yoga, adoration and worship are only the first stage of turning the heart and mind toward the Divine. The Yogin then begins a process of transforming his inner life to become a fit vessel of the Divine Presence. This is a process of consecration of the being, which starts by preparing the being to hold the higher energy of the Divine without "spilling" it in an unprepared system. This involves purification of the physical, vital, nervous, emotional and mental levels of the being.

When people consider purification, they generally associate it with outer cleansing, and some kind of ethical or moral code that is to be practiced. These are basic elements, but the true purification is one that is neither bound nor limited by externally developed moral or ethical codes; rather it involves a systematic and comprehensive approach toward aligning all the thoughts, emotions, energies and physical actions of the being towards the Divine and releasing all other motives and energies so that they no longer can disrupt or trouble the being.

Sri Aurobindo observes: "And one element of this consecration must be a self-purifying so as to become fit for the divine contact, or for the entrance of the Divine into the temple of our inner being, or for his self-revelation in the shrine of the heart. This purifying may be ethical in its character, but it will not be merely the moralist's seeking for the right and blameless action or even, when once we reach the stage of Yoga, an obedience to the law of God as revealed in formal religion; but it will be a throwing away, *katharsis*, of all that conflicts whether with the idea of the Divine in himself or of the Divine in ourselves. In the former case it becomes in habit of feeling and outer act an imitation of the Divine, in the latter a growing into his likeness in our nature. What inner adoration is to ceremonial worship, this growing into the divine likeness is to the outward ethical life. It culminates in a sort of liberation by likeness to the Divine, a liberation from our lower nature and a change into the divine nature."

Sri Aurobindo, The Synthesis of Yoga, Part Three: The Yoga of Divine Love, Chapter 4, The Way of Devotion, pp. 547-548

The Complete Self-Giving of an Integral Approach to Bhakti Yoga

The fullness of devotion leads eventually to the consecration of all the being to the Divine. The thoughts must be turned in that direction; the Will in works must carry out all actions dedicated to and as a sacrifice to the Divine. For the Bhakta, this is a natural result of the expression of love for the Divine.

Sri Aurobindo observes: "It is a sacrifice of life and works to the Divine, but a sacrifice of love more than a turning of the will to the divine Will. The Bhakta offers up his life and all that he is and all that he has and all that he does to the Divine. This surrender may take the ascetic form, as when he leaves the ordinary life of men and devotes his days solely to prayer and praise and worship or to ecstatic meditation, gives up his personal possessions and becomes the monk or the mendicant whose one only possession is the Divine, gives up all actions in life except those only which help or belong to the communion with the Divine and communion with other devotees, or at most keeps the doing, from the secure fortress of the ascetic life, of those services to men which seem peculiarly the outflowing of the divine nature of love, compassion and good."

For the seeker of the integral Yoga, this restricted focus of the life energy is not the final stage of the consecration. "But there is the wider self-consecration, proper to any integral Yoga, which, accepting the fullness of life and the world in its entirety as the play of the Divine, offers up the whole being into his possession; it is a holding of all one is and has as belonging to him only and not to ourselves and a doing of all works as an offering to him. By this comes the complete active consecration of both the inner and the outer life, the unmutilated self-giving."

Sri Aurobindo, The Synthesis of Yoga, Part Three: The Yoga of Divine Love, Chapter 4, The Way of Devotion, pp. 548-549

The Practice of Devotion in the Mind

In the Yoga of Knowledge, there is a focus in the mind on the Absolute and an abandonment of all the preoccupations or distractions of the outer world in order to achieve Oneness in the silence of the Beyond. In the Yoga of Devotion there can be a somewhat similar focus, insofar as the mind is asked to turn towards the Divine, fix itself on the Divine and become immersed in the ecstatic bliss of union with the Divine. The motive force here, however, is coming from the emotional nature of the devotee, and the goal sought is not some austere silent immutable Self, but a complete union with the Divine that fills the being with bliss.

Traditionally there are stages that are recognized in this pursuit, as described by Sri Aurobindo: "There are supposed by those who systematise, to be three stages of the seeking through the devotion of the mind, first, the constant hearing of the divine name, qualities and all that has been attached to them, secondly, the constant thinking on them or on the divine being or personality, thirdly, the settling and fixing of the mind on the object; and by this comes the full realisation."

Sri Aurobindo observes that these steps are not actually the essential principle: "the one thing essential is the intense devotion of the thought in the mind to the object of adoration."

While the seeker may go through various phases, including one of withdrawal from action in the world to focus on the Divine realisation, eventually the seeker can see that the Divine Being is everywhere and in all things, "all this is the Brahman" as the Upanishad so aptly puts it, and this changes the relation of the seeker to the universal manifestation: "As in the other Yogas, so in this, one comes to see the Divine everywhere and in all and to pour out the realisation of the Divine in all one's inner activities and outward actions. But all is supported here by the primary force of the emotional union: for it is by love that the entire self-consecration and the entire possession is accomplished, and thought and action become shapes and figures of the divine love which possesses the spirit and its members."

Sri Aurobindo, The Synthesis of Yoga, Part Three: The Yoga of Divine Love, Chapter 4, The Way of Devotion, pp. 549-550

Possessed by the Call of the Divine Flute Player

The natural tendency of the human mind is to try to create some kind of system or organized methdology that one can follow to achieve a particular result. This tendency carries through into the search for the Divine as well. Those who follow the path of devotion may, particularly in early stages, rely on specific habitual practices or rituals or modes of worship. The direct path to the divine through Bhakti Yoga, however, requires no system, no rules, no fixed methodology.

In the Bhagavad Gita, Sri Krishna explains this secret to Arjuna, that when he gives up all rules of life and turns his entire heart and soul toward the divine completely, the result is assured. No religious practice, no form of worship, no specific set of moral rules, no specific type of meditation, no prescribed outer form of action is required in such a case.

Sri Aurobindo observes: "But there is the more intimate Yoga which from the first consists in this love and attains only by the intensity of its longing without other process or method. All the rest comes but it comes out of this, as leaf and flower out of the seed; other things are not the means of developing and fulfilling love, but the radiations of love already growing in the soul.

This is the way that the soul follows when, while occupied perhaps with the normal human life, it has heard the flute of the Godhead behind the near screen of secret woodlands and no longer possesses itself, can have no satisfaction or rest till it has pursued and seized and possessed the divine flute-player. This is in essence the power of love itself in the heart and soul turning from earthly objects to the spiritual source of all beauty and delight."

When the seeker is entirely possessed by this intensity of love for the Divine, all the various manifestations of love play across his heart. "The heart is the scene of this supreme idyll of the inner consciousness, but a heart which undergoes increasingly an intense spiritual change and becomes the radiantly unfolding lotus of the spirit. And as the intensity of its seeking is beyond the highest power of the normal human emotions, so also the delight and the final ecstasy are beyond the reach of the imagination and beyond expression by speech. For this is the delight of the Godhead that passes human understanding."

The Taittirya Upanishad calls it "The Bliss of the Eternal from which words turn back without attaining and mind also returneth baffled…"

Sri Aurobindo, The Synthesis of Yoga, Part Three: The Yoga of Divine Love, Chapter 4, The Way of Devotion, pp. 550-551

The Heaven of Beatitude of the Eternal Union

The mystery of the divine Personality underlies the practice of the Yoga of devotion, and it is this divine Personality who is the object of the love and devotion in all the various forms that such love and devotion can take for the seeker. It is impossible to fully describe the experience of this relationship, so human thought and expression clothes it in the terms of human forms of love. Where human love, however, is found to be weak or imperfect, the divine Beloved is able to exceed and perfect the expression and inner sense of love.

Bhakti Yoga does not seek after the Absolute, silent, immutable and austere; rather, it fixes itself upon the personal aspect of the Divine as he manifests through all forms in the universal existence. The Shwetashwatara Upanishad calls out: "Thou art the woman and Thou the man; Thou art a boy and again a young virgin; Thou art yonder worn and aged man that walkest bent with thy staff. Lo, Thou becomest born and the world is full of thy faces." (Sri Aurobindo, *The Upanishads*, Shwetashwatara Upanishad, Chapter 4, v. 3, pg. 369)

Sri Aurobindo declares: "It is a living Soul to which the soul of the Bhakta yearns; for the source of all life is not an idea or a conception or a state of existence, but a real Being. Therefore in the possession of the divine Beloved all the life of the soul is satisfied and all the relations by which it finds and in which it expresses itself, are wholly fulfilled; therefore, too, by any and all of them can the Beloved be sought, though those which admit the greatest intensity, are always those by which he can be most intensely pursued and possessed with the profoundest ecstasy. He is sought within in the heart and therefore apart from all by an inward-gathered concentration of the being in the soul itself; but he is also seen and loved everywhere where he manifests his being. All the beauty and joy of existence is seen as his joy and beauty; he is embraced by the spirit in all beings; the ecstasy of love enjoyed pours itself out in a universal love; all existence becomes a radiation of its delight and even in its very appearances is transformed into something other than its outward appearance. The world itself is experienced as a play of the divine Delight, a Lila, and that in which the world loses itself is the heaven of beatitude of the eternal union."

Sri Aurobindo, The Synthesis of Yoga, Part Three: The Yoga of Divine Love, Chapter 4, The Way of Devotion, pg. 551

CHAPTER FIVE

THE DIVINE PERSONALITY

The Question of the Divine Personality

For those who follow a path of religion that believes in a personal God, the question of the Divine Personality is one of faith. In today's world, with its emphasis on facts, science and provable assumptions, the concept of a Divine Personality has been either entirely removed or relegated to the status of something illusory and less "real" than the Eternal, Impersonal, the Absolute. Western science, with its enormous analytical powers, has delved into the inner workings of the universal manifestation and found that there is an incredibly precise and balanced machinery of existence that constitutes forms and forces according to certain principles.

There are mathematical relationships that clearly control the relationships between forms. The Indian focus on the Yoga of Knowledge, coming at the issue from a different direction, found that form and personality were less real than the abstract, infinite and eternal consciousness which appeared to be highly impersonal. With respect to the Western approach, the emphasis has always been on analysis and the need to divide, categorize and segment everything into parts, so much so, that nowadays we are beginning to recognize that, as the proverb goes, they have "failed to see the forest for the trees."

The argument against a Divine Personality is based on this analysis of the view of an impersonal mechanism, a natural series of processes that carry out the functions of the machinery without any visible sign of a conscious personality involved in the result. The argument however always stops short of taking up the larger question of how this obviously precisely formed and intelligent universal creation came about and for what purpose. Where there is intelligence in the forms and their interactions, the question must be asked, as to how it got there, and who or what designed it. Once we come to this question it is clear that there must be a Divine Intelligence.

The next step is to determine to what degree that Divine Intelligence has made itself manifest as a Divine Personality.

Sri Aurobindo emphasizes the issue in the modern world: "All the trend of modern thought has been towards the belittling of personality; it has seen behind the complex facts of existence only a great impersonal force, an obscure becoming, and that too works itself out through impersonal forces and impersonal laws, while personality presents itself only as a subsequent, subordinate, partial, transient phenomenon upon the face of this impersonal movement."

This question must be answered in order to provide a solid basis for any Yoga of Devotion.

Sri Aurobindo, The Synthesis of Yoga, Part Three: The Yoga of Divine Love, Chapter 5, The Divine Personality, pp. 552-553

The Limitations of the Human Intellect In Perceiving the Ultimate Truths of Existence

Even the rational intellect can recognize that the human mind is unable to directly cognize and assimilate the entirety of the manifested universe. As humanity pushes ever farther in its examination of the facts of existence, this principle becomes ever more clear. We now know that the range of perceptions we have is limited both on the top and the bottom end, while other beings have the ability to perceive within different ranges, including some which are hidden from us. Just as we can recognize the limitations of the senses and the sense experience, we also have begun to recognize that forces at work which cannot be directly perceived, necessarily, but which have specific visible effects. This recognition of invisible forces which can be harnessed to our needs has led to the development of the theories of gravitation, the electro-magnetic spectrum and wireless transmission of energy and content. The laws of physics regarding momentum and inertia, and eventually the atomic theory which has brought about the ability to convert matter into energy are examples of forces outside the direct cognizance of our senses which nevertheless can be seen to exist. Quantum mechanics goes further in describing existence in ways that our senses would, at first, tend to deny. Similarly, exploration into biological processes shows us how our knowledge of the physiology of life is lacking.

The limiting intelligence of the mind has a similar inability to recognize higher realms of consciousness that nevertheless not only must be at work for the creation to exist in the first place, but which can be experienced through other means than the intellect. It is here that the spiritual intuition comes in to validate the truths of our existence that the mind cannot, at this stage of its development, prove to exist.

Sri Aurobindo observes: Spiritual intuition is always a more luminous guide than the discriminating reason, and spiritual intuition addresses itself to us not only through the reason, but through the rest of our being as well, through the heart and life also. The integral knowledge will then be that which takes account of all and unifies their diverse truths. The intellect itself will be more deeply satisfied if it does not confine itself to its own data, but accepts truth of the heart and the life also and gives to them their absolute spiritual value."

Sri Aurobindo, The Synthesis of Yoga, Part Three: The Yoga of Divine Love, Chapter 5, The Divine Personality, pg. 553

The Nature of the Philosophical Intellect

It is important to understand the human intellect, its capacities and its limitations, in order to get at the root cause of the disconnect that has generally taken place between the path of knowledge, the path of love and the path of works. The latter two are rooted in energies of life, while the mind has the capability of abstracting itself from life. This differentiating factor has caused the path of knowledge to move always further into abstractions, which has the effect of divorcing it from life and life-energies.

Sri Aurobindo explains: "The nature of the philosophical intellect is to move among ideas and to give them a sort of abstract reality of their own apart from all their concrete representations which affect our life and personal consciousness. Its bent is to reduce these representations to their barest and most general tems and to subtilise even these if possible into some final abstraction. The pure intellectual direction travels away from life."

Eventually the intellect comes to the conclusion that the most abstract formulation is the ultimate truth and all the external life and circumstances are somehow just incidents and thus, less "real".

The abstractions "existence", "consciousness" and "bliss" represented one such attempt to satisfy the intellect's need for some ultimate form of unchanging truth. As Sri Aurobindo describes it, this direction had to eventually "...throw all back into a pure featureless existence from which everything else had been discharged, all representations, all values, except the one infinite and timeless fact of being."

The intellect could even find a further abstraction by treating this timeless, unchanging existence as "only a representation; it abstracted that also and got to an infinite zero which might be either a void or an eternal inexpressible."

Sri Aurobindo, The Synthesis of Yoga, Part Three: The Yoga of Divine Love, Chapter 5, The Divine Personality, pp. 553-554

The Nature of the Heart and the Life-Force and Their Spiritual Fulfilment

Just as the intellect seeks abstraction, the heart and life-energy want to experience the reality in palpable terms. They are unable to grasp abstraction; they want to have the concrete experience and have it express itself through and in the life.

The Taittiriya Upanishad has an interesting passage wherein it distinguishes between those who focus on the abstract and the austere way of abandonment of the life for union with the Absolute versus those who focus on the realisation in the manifested universe: "One becometh as the unexisting, if he know the Eternal as negation; but if one knoweth of the Eternal that He is, then men know him for the saint and the one reality." (Sri Aurobindo, *The Upanishads*, Taittiriya Upanishad, Brahmanandavalli, ch. 6, pg. 270)

Sri Aurobindo observes: "Nor is it the satisfaction of an abstract mind or impersonal existence to which they respond, but the joy and the activity of a being, a conscious Person in us, whether finite or infinite, to whom the delights and powers of his existence are a reality. Therefore when the heart and life turn towards the Highest and the Infinite, they arrive not at an abstract existence or non-existence, a Sat or else a Nirvana, but at an existent, a Sat Purusha, not merely at a consciousness, but at a conscious Being, a Chaitanya Purusha, not merely at a purely impersonal delight of the Is, but at an infinite I Am of bliss, an Anandamaya Purusha; nor can they immerge and lose his consciousness and bliss in featureless existence, but must insist on all three in one, for delight of existence is their highest power and without consciousness delight cannot be possessed. That is the sense of the supreme figure of the intensest Indian religion of love, Sri Krishna, the All-blissful and All-beautiful."

Sri Aurobindo, The Synthesis of Yoga, Part Three: The Yoga of Divine Love, Chapter 5, The Divine Personality, pp. 554-555

The Impersonal and the Personal Aspects of Reality

The intellect struggles to understand existence. Due to the structure of the mind, it tends to adopt an exclusive position and deny the validity or truth of an opposing view. Thus, we see that different aspects of the integral Reality appeal to the intellect in different ways. For those who fix themselves on the Impersonal, they treat the Unmanifest, the Infinite, the Absolute, the Eternal as unmoving and without qualities, *Nirguna*. Sri Aurobindo declares: "Therefore the severest intellectual philosophy admits the Saguna, the divine Person, only as the supreme cosmic symbol; go beyond it to reality and you will arrive, it says, at last to the Nirguna, the pure Impersonal."

There is however, another view that comes to the questions of existence from the other end, so to speak. In this view, it is the Saguna, the Divine Personality, the manifested universal creation, that is ultimately the "real" and the Nirguna is the substrate that is void of all qualities out of which the manifestation arises. "...that which is impersonal is, it will perhaps say, only the material, the stuff of his spiritual nature out of which he manifests the powers of his being, consciousness and bliss, all that expresses him; the impersonal is the apparent negative out of which he looses the temporal variations of his eternal positive of personality."

From an integral perspective, both the Impersonal and the Personal, the Nirguna as well as the Saguna, are aspects of one and the same integral truth, which Sri Aurobindo elsewhere calls "Reality Omnipresent."

Sri Aurobindo, The Synthesis of Yoga, Part Three: The Yoga of Divine Love, Chapter 5, The Divine Personality, pg. 555

The Need to Integrate the Truths of the Intellect With the Truths of the Heart and Life

The human mind naturally moves towards an "either/or" paradigm. This means essentially that if one particular thing is considered true, the opposite must be considered false. While this works for the logical intellect within certain fixed limits within the world of forms and forces, it clearly is unable to encompass the diversity, complexity and immensity of the universal creation or the process or origin of its creation.

It is also possible to take one side of the argument while someone else equally supports the other side, and each of them relies on certain aspects of the truth of things to support their opposing positions.

In *The Life Divine,* Sri Aurobindo explores the dichotomy between the view of the "materialist" and that of the "ascetic". Each one relies on certain facts to bolster their individual viewpoints; yet there is a larger synthesis or harmony possible that recognizes the truth that supports both of these apparently contradictory, but in reality complementary, positions. This is "reality omnipresent" which accepts both the Impersonal and the Personal as equally real and equally an aspect of the Divine.

"Both the ideas of the intellect, its discriminations, and the aspirations of the heart and life, their approximations, have behind them realities at which they are the means of arriving. Both are justified by spiritual experience; both arrive at the divine absolute of that which they are seeking. But still each tends, if too exclusively indulged, to be hampered by the limitations of its innate quality and its characteristic means. We see that in our earthly living where the heart and life followed exclusively failed to lead to any luminous issue, while an exclusive intellectuality becomes either remote, abstract and impotent or a sterile critic or dry mechanist. Their sufficient harmony and just reconciliation is one of the great problems of our psychology and our action."

Sri Aurobindo, The Synthesis of Yoga, Part Three: The Yoga of Divine Love, Chapter 5, The Divine Personality, pg. 555

The Intuition As an Integral Truth-Finder

As long as the seeker is bound within the limitations of the instruments of body, life and mind, he is unable to perceive and respond to another level of conscious awareness. In order to overpass the limits of these instruments, another power must accessible to the seeker and then must be called upon. That power is the intuition. Intuition may act at the level of the mind, or at the level of the heart or life or even the physical body. We get a "sense" of something that cannot be explained with the logical intellect as a direct and identifiable perception. To the extent that we focus the intuition on the specific power, either mind, emotions, life energy or body, it remains circumscribed as well. The true power of the intuition comes when it is unhooked from the specific control of one particular power or plane of existence and can take up the task of seeking out the truth of things in whatever realm of existence it is called upon.

Sri Aurobindo discusses this issue: "But the fact that it can lend itself impartially to all parts of our being,–for even the body has its intuitions,–shows that the intuition is not exclusive, but an integral truth-finder. We have to question the intuition of our whole being, not only separately in each part of it, nor in a sum of their findings, but beyond all these lower instruments, beyond even their first spiritual correspondents, by rising into the native home of the intuition which is the native home of the infinite and infallible Truth..., where all existence discovers its unity."

The implication here is that intuition has its own plane of action where it is both native and unfettered by the limitations of body, life-energy and mind, and when we attain to that plane and thereby receive the native action of the intuition, we can then experience the truth that unifies those things which, at the level of mind, life and body, seem fragmented, disjointed and divided from one another.

Sri Aurobindo, The Synthesis of Yoga, Part Three: The Yoga of Divine Love, Chapter 5, The Divine Personality, pp. 555-556

Spiritual Intuition and the One Reality

The faculty of spiritual intuition possesses a certainty and insight which are missing from the mind, heart and vital sense. Everyone is familiar with various forms of intuition and have experienced from time to time a certainty that something was going to occur, or that something was wrong. Some people describe this as some kind of physical sensation in their midsection, what they might call a "gut instinct". Sometimes, if it is in the mind, it is recognized as a flash of awareness that does not follow the plodding steps of the rational intellect, yet one knows and feels the "rightness" of the insight. The unique quality of spiritual intuition is that it exceeds both the mental and the vital-physical forms of knowledge and is able to do what neither of them can do: grasp the unity and complementary nature of the rigid determinations of either the mind on one side, or the heart and life on the other.

Sri Aurobindo observes: "The spiritual intuition lays hold always upon the reality; it is the luminous harbinger of spiritual realisation or else its illuminative light; it sees that which the other powers of our being are labouring to explore; it gets at the firm truth of the abstract representations of the intellect and the phenomenal representations of the heart and life, a truth which is itself neither remotely abstract nor outwardly concrete, but something else for which these are only two sides of its psychological manifestation to us. What the intuition of our integral being perceives, when its members no longer dispute among themselves but are illumined from above, is that the whole of our being aims at the one reality. The impersonal is a truth, the personal too is a truth; they are the same truth seen from two sides of our psychological activity; neither by itself gives the total account of the Reality and yet by either we can approach it."

Sri Aurobindo, The Synthesis of Yoga, Part Three: The Yoga of Divine Love, Chapter 5, The Divine Personality, pg. 556

Two Parallel Lines Meeting In Infinity

The human individual has the capability to view his existence from a variety of standpoints. If he starts from the Impersonal, he can look up the thoughts of the mind, the will and action of the vital force and the emotions of the heart as some kind of created fiction, an illusion, not a reality. In this instance, he focuses on the Impersonal Existence, the Impersonal Consciousness and the Impersonal Bliss as the sole reality and works to overcome the illusory distractions of the outer world.

It is also possible, however, for the human individual to take his standpoint in the Personal. In this instance, it is the individual's thoughts, actions, emotions which are real, and the Impersonal can be seen as the illusion.

The seeker of the integral Yoga recognizes that each of these divergent standpoints has its own truth, but that neither one, on its own, represents the entire truth; rather, they are complementary truths that must be fused together in order for a comprehensive truth to manifest for the seeker.

Sri Aurobindo observes: "Both views are true, except that the idea of fiction, which is borrowed from our own intellectual processes, has to be exiled and each must be given its proper validity. The integral seeker has to see in this light that he can reach one and the same Reality on both lines, either successively or simultaneously, as if on two connected wheels travelling on parallel lines, but parallel lines which in defiance of intellectual logic but in obedience to their own inner truth of unity do meet in infinity."

Sri Aurobindo, The Synthesis of Yoga, Part Three: The Yoga of Divine Love, Chapter 5, The Divine Personality, pp. 556-557

Conceptions About the Divine Personality

When the individual considers the idea of "personality", even a Divine Personality, he begins by relating it to what is already known to him. Therefore, the first conceptions of Divine Personality take on characteristics similar to those of the human personality. Sri Aurobindo observes: "Our personality is to us at first a separate creature, a limited mind, body, character which we conceive of as the person we are, a fixed quantity; for although in reality it is always changing, yet there is a sufficient element of stability to give a kind of practical justification to this notion of fixedness. We conceive of God as such a person, only without body, a separate person different from all others with a mind and character limited by certain qualities."

Our limited experience of personality then attributes the same kind of characteristics as we see within ourselves to our personal idea of God. In some cases, God is seen as vindictive and vengeful; in others, lustful and jealous, and yet in others, subject to flattery and propitiation. And of course God also takes on characteristics of benign affection, goodwill and helpfulness at times.

As the human mind progresses in its conceptualisation of God, it begins to attribute unlimited qualities to God, such as omniscience, omnipotence, and all-loving, all-seeing goodwill. A problem then arises when we compare this conception with what we experience in the world. When we see evil, or suffering, we find it impossible to reconcile these things with our all-knowing, all-compassionate Divine Personality. It is at this point that we begin to propose alternatives such as the devil to be the embodiment of evil and the opposite or antagonist to God. Or we may try to distinguish between all-good in the form of God, versus an independent Nature that allows of weakness, limitation and suffering.

"At a higher pitch the attribution of mind and character to God becomes less anthropomorphic and we regard him as an infinite Spirit, but still a separate person, a spirit with certain fixed divine qualities as his attributes. So are conceived the ideas of the divine Personality, the personal God which vary so much in various religions."

Sri Aurobindo, The Synthesis of Yoga, Part Three: The Yoga of Divine Love, Chapter 5, The Divine Personality, pp. 557-558

Monotheism, Polytheism and the Divine Personality

The original anthropomorphic concepts of the Divine have been subjected to intense intellectual scrutiny by the analytical mind. In fact, much of the modern day debate between science and religion stems from the debunking of some of the more juvenile conceptions that arose in the development of the idea of a personal God. Sri Aurobindo observes: "It is not surprising that the philosophical and sceptical mind should have found little difficulty in destroying it all intellectually, whether in the direction of the denial of a personal God and the assertion of an impersonal Force or Becoming or in that of an impersonal Being or an ineffable denial of existence with all the rest as only symbols of Maya or phenomenal truths of the Time-consciousness. But these are only the personifications of monotheism." The very idea of one supreme God, sitting on some heavenly throne, and dispensing out judgments on each individual being for acts that were more or less pre-determined by that selfsame God, is difficult for the modern mind to accept.

There are, however, also various polytheistic religions. They may accept the idea of some supreme form or conscious existence, but they also see the divinity in all things, and in most cases, personify the consciousness of each thing as a divinity. "...but where the inner sense of spiritual things became clearer, the various godheads assumed the appearance of personalities of the one Divine,–that is the declared point of view of the ancient Veda. This Divine might be a supreme Being who manifests himself in various divine personalities or an impersonal existence which meets the human mind in these forms; or both views might be held simultaneously without any intellectual attempt to reconcile them, since both were felt to be true to spiritual experience."

Obviously the modern mind of science has an equally hard time accepting the concepts of polytheism; however, the polytheists have a spiritual sense of the Oneness of all existence, and the divine nature of Reality which carries the weight of truth once the doors of spiritual experience have begun to open and the seeker sees with the spiritual intuition or the Divine sight.

Sri Aurobindo, The Synthesis of Yoga, Part Three: The Yoga of Divine Love, Chapter 5, The Divine Personality, pp. 558-559

Spiritual Experience and the Divine Personality

It would be a mistake to allow the logical intellect of the mind to act as the sole judge and jury of the truth of any particular view of existence. Despite its arrogant insistence on its scientific, fact-based, approach, this mental power is only able to perceive and act within a certain limited range or experience and has, as its fundamental method, a method that seeks out differences and points of separation rather than finds the underlying unity and the established Oneness. To the extent this intellect begins to recognize the inherent Unity of all existence, with concepts such as biosphere, ecosphere, noosphere, it begins also to recognize that there are aspects of existence far outside its own boundaries of action and thus, it needs to cede its judgment to other forms of knowing. Spiritual experience and spiritual intuition are a different type of knwoing, one that bases its knowledge on a sense of identify.

The mind, when confronted with the concept of a divine Personality, simply is unable to comprehend, and tends to treat this as Sri Aurobindo describes, as "...fictions of the imagination or to psychological symbols, in any case, the responses of our sensitive personality to something which is not this at all, but is purely impersonal. We may say that That is in reality the very opposite of our humanity and our personality and therefore in order to enter into relations with it we are impelled to set up these human fictions and these personal symbols so as to make it nearer to us."

"But we have to judge by spiritual experience, and in a total spiritual experience we shall find that these things are not fictions and symbols, but truths of divine being in their essence, however imperfect may have been our representations of them....Greater self-knowledge shows us that we are not fundamentally the particular formulation of form, powers, properties, qualities with a conscious I identifying itself with them, which we at first appear to be. That is only a temporary fact, though still a fact, of our partial being on the surface of our active consciousness. We find within an infinite being with the potentiality of all qualities, of infinite quality, *anantaguna*, which can be combined in any number of possible ways, and each combination is a revelation of our being. For all this personality is the self-manifestation of a Person, that is to say, of a being who is conscious of his manifestation."

Sri Aurobindo, The Synthesis of Yoga, Part Three: The Yoga of Divine Love, Chapter 5, The Divine Personality, pg. 559

Forms of the Divine Personality

When the cells that comprise the foot reflect on their existence, it is likely that they wonder whether there is an divine Being or Personality of which they are a portion, or if they are all alone in the universe, having to interact with other cells in their neighborhood and somehow learning to get along with one another while carrying out their purpose of existence, in whatever way they conceive that purpose. They may come to conclude that there is a larger unified whole and some controlling force of their existence, although they may decide, particularly when the toe gets stubbed, or the foot steps on a sharp rock, that perhaps there is no higher conscious existence, or if there is, that the suffering is there for some purpose. Or they may determine that such suffering is some kind of karmic retribution for mistakes it made in the past.

Seriously, however, putting aside the question of the foot as a portion of a larger conscious being, we are faced with a quite similar situation when we try to interact with the forms of the divine Personality. There are frames of awareness where the conscious being seems to disappear and the universe takes on the appearance of some "timeless pure existence." It can go even further, as Sri Aurobindo explains: "And again even this pure self of our being seems at a certain pitch to deny its own reality, or to be a projection from a selfless baseless unknowable, which we may conceive of either as a nameless somewhat, or as a Nihil." For the seeker who fixates his attention on this aspect, the idea of divine Personality becomes impossible to conceive: "It is when we would fix upon this exclusively and forget all that it has withdrawn into itself that we speak of pure impersonality or the void Nihil as the highest truth."

The seeker of the integral Yoga, however, focuses on the synthesis of the Impersonal and the Personal aspect and recognizes that even this impersonal standpoint is but an aspect of the divine conscious Being who creates and sustains the entire universal creation in all its forms, forces, and actions. "And if we carry up our heart as well as our reasoning mind to the Highest, we shall find that we can reach it through the absolute Person as well as through an absolute impersonality."

"But all this self-knowledge is only the type within ourselves of the corresponding truth of the Divine in his universality. There too we meet him in various forms of divine personality; in formulations of quality which variously express him to us in his nature; in infinite quality, the Anantaguna; in the divine Person who expresses himself through infinite quality; in absolute impersonality, an absolute existence or an absolute non-existence, which is yet all the time the unexpressed Absolute of this divine Person, this conscious Being who manifests himself through us and through the universe."

Sri Aurobindo, The Synthesis of Yoga, Part Three: The Yoga of Divine Love, Chapter 5, The Divine Personality, pp. 559-560

The Universal Divine Conscious Being: The Purushottama

In the Bhagavad Gita, Sri Krishna declares: "Since I am beyond the mutable and am greater and higher even than the immutable, in the world and the Veda I am proclaimed as the Purushottama (the supreme Self). (Sri Aurobindo, *Bhagavad Gita and Its Message*, Chapter 15, v. 18)

Due to the natural tendency of the mind, we like to create abstractions and symbols to define for ourselves the nature of the divine reality. Thus, we attach to our conception of the Divine, various abstract principles. Sri Aurobindo observes: "We may think, feel and say that God is Truth, Justice, Righteousness, Power, Love, Delight, Beauty; we may see him as a universal force or as a universal consciousness."

At the same time, we recognize within ourselves something other than a collection of abstract principles, something we identify as personality. "...so is the Divine a Person, a conscious Being who thus expresses his nature to us."

With such a vision, we must be prepared to see both those qualities that we identify positively, and those that we identify negative. The Divine manifests in all his complexity, in ways that our limited human understanding cannot fully fathom. "He is Vishnu, Krishna, Kali; he reveals himself to us in humanity as the Christ personality or the Buddha personality. When we look beyond our first exclusively concentrated vision, we see behind Vishnu all the personality of Shiva and behind Shiva all the personality of Vishnu. He is the Ananta-guna, infinite quality and the infinite divine Personality which manifests itself through it. Again he seems to withdraw into a pure spiritual impersonality or beyond all idea even of impersonal Self and to justify a spiritualised atheism or agnosticism; he becomes to the mind of man an indefinable.... But out of this unknowable the conscious Being, the divine Person, who has manifested himself here, still speaks, 'This too is I; even here beyond the view of mind, I am He, the Purushottama.' "

In conclusion: "For, beyond the divisions and contradictions of the intellect there is another light and there the vision of a truth reveals itself which we may thus try to express to ourselves intellectually. There all is one truth of all these truths; for there each is present and justified in all the rest. In that light our spiritual experience becomes united and integralised; no least hair's breadth of real division is left, no shade of superiority and inferiority remains between the seeking of the Impersonal and the adoration of the divine Personality, between the way of knowledge and the way of devotion."

The Upanishadic dicta remind us "One without a second", while at the same time "All this is the Brahman."

Sri Aurobindo, The Synthesis of Yoga, Part Three: The Yoga of Divine Love, Chapter 5, The Divine Personality, pp. 560-561

CHAPTER SIX

THE DELIGHT OF THE DIVINE

Understanding Our Spiritual Destiny

Sri Aurobindo observes: "Yoga is in essence the union of the soul with the immortal being and consciousness and delight of the Divine, effected through the human nature with a result of development into the divine nature of being, whatever that may be, so far as we can conceive it in mind and realise it in spiritual activity."

When we focus our attention on any particular aspect of the Divine, we enter into a relationship with that aspect and are thereby able to move our consciousness in that direction and take on the characteristics of that aspect. The Taittiriya Upanishad advises: "Pursue thou Him as the firm foundation of things and thou shalt get thee firm foundation; pursue Him as Mahas, thou shalt become Mighty; pursue him as Mind, thou shalt become full of mind; pursue Him as adoration, thy desires shall bow down before thee; pursue Him as the Eternal, thou shalt become full of the Spirit; pursue Him as the destruction of the Eternal that rangeth abroad, thy rivals and thy haters shall perish thick around thee and thy kin who loveth thee not." (Sri Aurobindo, *The Upanishads*, Taittiriya Upanishad, Brahmanandavalli, ch. 10, pg. 281)

Sri Aurobindo summarizes: "...that, we may say, is at once the essential and the pragmatic truth of the Godhead. It is something beyond us which is indeed already within us, but which we as yet are not or are only initially in our human existence; but whatever of it we see, we can create or reveal in our conscious nature and being and can grow into it, and so to create or reveal in ourselves individually the Godhead and grow into its universality and transcendence is our spiritual destiny. Or if this seems too high for the weakness of our nature, then at least to approach, reflect and be in secure communion with it is a near and possible consummation."

Sri Aurobindo, The Synthesis of Yoga, Part Three: The Yoga of Divine Love, Chapter 6, The Delight of the Divine, pg. 562

Understanding the Comprehensive Aim of the Integral Yoga

Each path of Yoga has its own aims and methodology. For some it is immersion in the impersonal Absolute; for others it is becoming the perfect implement of a divine action; and for yet others, it is the intensity of love and devotion that comes from a deep union with the personal Divine. The seeker of the integral Yoga looks for a complete transformation of the life at all levels and in all parts of the being. All of the realisations that are part of the more specialized paths are to be incorporated into the integral approach.

Sri Aurobindo observes: "The aim of this synthetic or integral Yoga which we are considering, is union with the being, consciousness and delight of the Divine through every part of our human nature separately or simultaneously, but all in the long end harmonised and unified, so that the whole may be transformed into a divine nature of being. Nothing less than this can satisfy the integral seer, because what he sees must be that which he strives to possess spiritually and, so far as may be, become."

"And since God meets us in many ways of his being and in all tempts us to him even while he seems to elude us,–and to see divine possibility and overcome its play of obstacles constitutes the whole mystery and greatness of human existence,–therefore in each of these ways at its highest or in the union of all, if we can find the key of their oneness, we shall aspire to track out and find and possess him. Since he withdraws into impersonality, we follow after his impersonal being and delight, but since he meets us also in our personality and through personal relations of the Divine with the human, that too we shall not deny ourselves; we shall admit both the play of the love and the delight and its ineffable union."

Sri Aurobindo, The Synthesis of Yoga, Part Three: The Yoga of Divine Love, Chapter 6, The Delight of the Divine, pp. 562-563

The Path of Love Supplies the Most Comprehensive Motive of Yoga

When we view the three main streams of yogic practice, knowledge, works and love, we find that each one has its own unique focus or motivation. Sri Aurobindo briefly describes the three: "By knowledge we seek unity with the Divine in his conscious being; by works we seek also unity with the Dviine in his conscious being, not statically, but dynamically, through conscious union with the divine Will; but by love we seek unity with him in all the delight of his being. For that reason the way of love, however narrow it may seem in some of its first movements, is in the end more imperatively all-embracing than any other motive of Yoga."

Sri Aurobindo goes on to explain that the way of knowledge may tend to focus itself away from life and manifestation as it seeks after the Impersonal and Absolute. While it may recognize the universality of the divine manifestation, yet this is only one branch of the practice of the yoga of knowledge. We see frequently a division between a "higher knowledge" and a "lower knowledge" with emphasis placed on the impersonal side rather than the aspect of the manifested world and our individual potential role in it.

Similarly, while the way of works apparently embraces the manifestation and the role of the individual, it may tend to do so in a passive manner as an impersonal actor with the end seen as the union, once again, with the Impersonal aspect of the Divine.

"It is only when delight intervenes that the motive of integral union becomes quite imperative."

The delight of the Divine encompasses relation with the entire manifested creation, participates in the universal creation and embraces all the individual aspects that make up that creation, understanding through a deep sense of Oneness and participation that the Divine is both the Impersonal, beyond all these creations, names and forms, and always free and above, and the Personal, entering into, interacting and constituting the entire universal manifestation through a deep sense of delight in the play and the action of the Divine Creation.

Sri Aurobindo, The Synthesis of Yoga, Part Three: The Yoga of Divine Love, Chapter 6, The Delight of the Divine, pp. 563-564

The Integral Delight in the Integral Yoga

When we reflect on the concept or experience of delight, it is usually associated with a specific set of circumstances or conditions. We delight in physical things and the experience of them. We delight in various vital and emotional relationships. We delight in mental results and we delight in psychic, spiritual and transcendent experiences. In each case, the delight is caused by and related to a specific causative thing or event.

Sri Aurobindo observes that there is a delight of existence that transcends and incorporates, while exceeding, all of these specific forms of delight. "A perfect and complete delight in the Divine, perfect because pure and self-existent, complete because all-embracing as well as all-absorbing, is the meaning of the way of Bhakti for the seeker of the integral Yoga."

He explains this in greater detail: "This delight which is so entirely imperative, is the delight in the Divine for his own sake and for nothing else, for no cause or gain whatever beyond itself. It does not seek God for anything that he can give us or for any particular quality in him, but simply and purely because he is our self and our whole being and our all. It embraces the delight of transcendence, not for the sake of transcendence, but because he is the transcendent; the delight of the universal, not for the sake of universality, but because he is the universal; the delight of the individual not for the sake of individual satisfaction, but because he is the individual."

"The integral delight embraces him not only within our own individual being, but equally in all men and in all beings. And because in him we are one with all, it seeks him not only for ourselves, but for all our fellows."

The delight of individual salvation, the delight of oneness with the Transcendent, the delight of any power, experience or acquisition in the material world is too partial and limited to satisfy the demand of the integral Yoga. The delight should be unconditional and unconditioned, experienced in all ways and aspects and parts of our being, and spread throughout all creation.

The Taittiriya Upanishad reveals the essence of this delight: "The Bliss of the Eternal from which words turn back without attaining and mind also returneth baffled, who knoweth the Bliss of the Eternal? He feareth not for aught in this world or elsewhere. Verily to him cometh not remorse and her torment saying, 'Why have i left undone the good and why have I done that which was evil?' For he who knoweth the Eternal, knoweth these that they are alike, and delivereth from them his Spirit; yea, he knoweth both evil and good for what they are and delivereth his Spirit, who knoweth the Eternal." (Sri Aurobindo, *The Upanishads*, Taittiriya Upanishad, Brahmanandavalli Ch. 9, pg. 274)

Sri Aurobindo, The Synthesis of Yoga, Part Three: The Yoga of Divine Love, Chapter 6, The Delight of the Divine, pp. 564-565

The God-Lover as the God-Knower

The mind tries to create an artificial separation between the paths of knowledge, works, and love. While each follows its own primary line of development, at a certain point they all can recognize the aspects of each other. For the seeker of the Yoga of love and devotion, the early stages may include an exclusive concentration on the heart and the emotional development of the nature, but eventually, the Bhakta can realize the truths of Oneness that accompany the practice of the Yoga of knowledge, as Sri Aurobindo observes:

"This integral devotion of our being to God does not turn away from knowledge; the Bhakta of this path is the God-lover who is also the God-knower, because by knowledge of his being comes the whole delight of his being; but is in delight that knowledge fulfils itself, the knowledge of the transcendent in the delight of the Transcendent, the knowledge of the universal in the delight of the universal Godhead, the knowledge of the individual manifestation in the delight of God in the individual, the knowledge of the impersonal in the pure delight of his impersonal being, the knowledge of the personal in the full delight of his personality, the knowledge of his qualities and their play in the delight of the manifestation, the knowledge of the qualityless in the delight of his colourless existence and non-manifestation."

Sri Aurobindo, The Synthesis of Yoga, Part Three: The Yoga of Divine Love, Chapter 6, The Delight of the Divine, pg. 565

The God-Lover as the Divine Worker

It is both easy, and understandable, that the Bhakta, enraptured in the emotional intensity of divine love, will seek to limit other activities and concentrate on the devotional acts which bring him closer to the Divine, and which intensifies the rapture of the embrace of God. As the identification with the Divine grows, however, it becomes possible to put aside this intense, limited focus and recognize that God is in all beings, all forms, all actions and is the mover and actor in all that occurs in the universe. It is also possible thereby to see that carrying out action in the world consistent with the Divine Will is itself an expression of devotion and can lead to the experience of the delight of manifesting the Divine intention.

Sri Aurobindo observes: "So too this God-lover will be the divine worker, not for the sake of works or for a self-regarding pleasure in action, but because in this way God expends the power of his being and in his powers and their signs we find him, because the divine Will in works is the outflowing of the Godhead in the delight of its power, of divine Being in the delight of divine Force."

"…when he works, he feels that he is expressing in act and power his oneness with that which he loves and adores; he feels the rapture of the will which he obeys and with which all the force of his being is blissfully identified."

Sri Aurobindo, The Synthesis of Yoga, Part Three: The Yoga of Divine Love, Chapter 6, The Delight of the Divine, pp. 565-566

The God-Lover as the Universal Lover

We seek for God outside our lives the world. We treat the world as something inferior and separate, something to be dismissed or abandoned if we want to find God. The devotee gives up his life in the world, is told to leave friends, family and worldly activities behind to focus on God-realisation. We observe the forms and forces in the world and treat them as if they are an obstacle to our devotion. Sri Aurobindo takes a different approach however. For him, the entire world, the entire universal manifestation is the face of God, the forms of God, the manifested becoming of God. The devotee can find God everywhere, in all things, in all events, in all beings. This opens up the secret of universal love and Ananda for the integral devotee.

"All Nature and all life will be to him at once a revelation and a fine trysting-place. Intellectual and aesthetic and dynamic activities, science and philosophy and life, thought and art and action will assume for him a diviner sanction and a greater meaning. He will seek them because of his clear sight of the Divine through them and because of the delight of the Divine in them."

"The general power of Delight is love and the special mould which the joy of love takes is the vision of beauty. The God-lover is the universal lover and he embraces the All-blissful and All-beautiful. When universal love has seized on his heart, it is the decisive sign that the Divine has taken possession of him; and when he has the vision of the All-beautiful everywhere and can feel at all times the bliss of his embrace, that is the decisive sign that he has taken possession of the Divine. Union is the consummation of love, but it is this mutual possession that gives it at once the acme and the largest reach of its intensity. It is the foundation of oneness in ecstasy."

Sri Aurobindo, The Synthesis of Yoga, Part Three: The Yoga of Divine Love, Chapter 6, The Delight of the Divine, pg. 566

CHAPTER SEVEN

THE ANANDA BRAHMAN

The Way of Devotion in the Integral Yoga

Whether the seeker in the integral path starts from the path of Knowledge, the path of Works or directly with the path of Love and Devotion, he will modify the traditional path to incorporate all aspects and elements of existence into his seeking. Sri Aurobindo explains:

"The way of devotion in the integral synthetic Yoga will take the form of a seeking after the Divine through love and delight and a seizing with joy on all the ways of his being. It will find its acme in a perfect union of love and a perfect enjoyment of all the ways of the soul's intimacy with God."

"It may start from knowledge or it may start from works, but it will then turn knowledge into a joy of luminous union with the being of the Beloved and turn works into a joy of the active union of our being with the will and the power of being of the Beloved. Or it may start directly from love and delight; it will then take both these other things into itself and will develop them as part of the complete joy of oneness."

Sri Aurobindo, The Synthesis of Yoga, Part Three: The Yoga of Divine Love, Chapter 7, The Ananda Brahman, pg. 567

Becoming Aware of the Ananda Brahman

Behind all the hustle and bustle of the daily routine, behind the joy and the sorrow, the pleasure and the pain that accompanies actions in the world, there is a Reality which is silent, unmoving, and yet holds an unchanging and unconditioned bliss of existence. There are moments in the life of the spiritual seeker where this realisation becomes paramount and one is in touch with this impersonal bliss, known in the texts as "Ananda" and it sustains the seeker in all circumstances.

The Taittiriya Upanishad references this experience: "Lo, this that is well and beautifully made, verily it is no other than the delight behind existence. When he hath gotten him this delight, then it is that this creature becometh a thing of bliss; for who could labour to draw in the breath or who could have strength to breathe it out, if there were not that Bliss in the heaven of his heart, the ether within his being?" (Sri Aurobindo, *The Upanishads*, Taittiriya Upanishad, Brahmanandavalli, Ch. 7, pg. 271)

Sri Aurobindo observes: "The beginning of the heart's attraction to the Divine may be impersonal, the touch of an impersonal joy in something universal or transcendent that has revealed itself directly or indirectly to our emotional or our aesthetic being or to our capacity of spiritual felicity. That which we thus grow aware of is the Ananda Brahman, the bliss existence. There is an adoration of an impersonal Delight and Beauty, of a pure and an infinite perfection to which we can give no name or form, a moved attraction of the soul to some ideal and infinite Presence, Power, existence in the world or beyond it, which in some way becomes psychologically or spiritually sensible to us and then more and more intimate and real. That is the call, the touch of the bliss existence upon us."

The soul so touched works to harmonize his inner and outer existence to this experience, and to find a way to live constantly in the presence of this ineffable bliss.

Sri Aurobindo, The Synthesis of Yoga, Part Three: The Yoga of Divine Love, Chapter 7, The Ananda Brahman, pp. 567-568

The Touch of the Divine Ananda

Divine bliss, Ananda, is a different order of experience from what we know as joy in the vital life in the world. The experience of joy arises when we feel that a desire has been met, whether it is a physical desire or need that has been satisfied, providing a sensation of physical joy, or a vital or emotional desire or need which provides the excitement of a vital joy; or the satisfaction of various mental achievements, which provides mental joy. The Taittiriya Upanishad posits the situation of the human individual, young, healthy, radiant, successful, all desires being met, and this is consider to be the measure of one "human bliss". It proceeds to show that there are numerous further levels of bliss, each one " a hundred and a hundredfold" greater than the preceding level. Interestingly each level of bliss is then equated with "the bliss of the vedawise, whose soul the blight of desire touches not." The Upanishad here is pointing the way for the seeker to come to the realisation of these higher states of Ananda which cannot be even remotely compared with the human experience of joy.

Sri Aurobindo elaborates: "But if the mind has once grown sufficiently subtle and pure in its receptions and not limited by the grosser nature of our outward responses to existence, we can take a reflection of it which will wear perhaps wholly or predominantly the hue of whatever is strongest in our nature. It may present itself first as a yearning for some universal Beauty which we feel in Nature and man and in all that is around us; or we may have the intuition of some transcendent Beauty of which all apparent beauty here is only a symbol. That is how it may come to those in whom the aesthetic being is developed and insistent and the instincts which, when they find form of expression, make the poet and artist, are predominant. Or it may be the sense of a divine spirit of love or else a helpful and compassionate infinite Presence in the universe or behind or beyond it which responds to us when we turn the need of our spirit towards it. So it may first show itself when the emotional being is intensely developed. It may come near to us in other ways, but always a Power or Presence of delight, beauty, love or peace which touches the mind, but is beyond the forms these things take ordinarily in the mind."

Sri Aurobindo, The Synthesis of Yoga, Part Three: The Yoga of Divine Love, Chapter 7, The Ananda Brahman, pg. 568

The Lower and the Higher Forms of Delight

The Divine is not separate from the manifested world, so we could expect to see the outpouring of the Divine Delight, Ananda, in the external world. Sri Aurobindo observes: "For all joy, beauty, love, peace, delight are outflowings from the Ananda Brahman,– all delight of the spirit, the intellect, the imagination, aesthetic sense, ethical aspiration and satisfaction, action, life, the body. And through all ways of our being the Divine can touch us and make use of them to awaken and liberate the spirit."

The joy and delight that we can experience in the external world, however, is a weak, filtered and inconsistent form of the Ananda, not the intensity and purity of Ananda in its native form and on its native plane. Just as existence is filtered into an inconstant struggle for life, with death as a constant process, and just as consciousness is filtered into an ignorance that attempts to gain knowledge through acquisition of bits and pieces of information and through extrapolation, so too Ananda, bliss, is filtered into the experience of joy and sorrow, pleasure and pain, satisfaction and dissatisfaction.

We live in a world that has consciousness deeply involved and embedded in Matter, and systematically evolving out into ever higher, purer and more powerful forms, through life, mind, and the supramental planes until we can identify with and experience the pure force of Sat-Chit-Ananda in the fully evolved soul. Each level of evolution is more refined, more subtle and more powerful than the one before it. This is the key to attaining the higher form of delight.

"But to reach the Ananda Brahman in itself the mental reception of it must be subtilised, spiritualised, universalised, discharged of everything that is turbid and limiting. For when we draw quite near or enter into it, it is by an awakened spiritual sense of a transcendent and a universal Delight which exists within and yet behind and beyond the contradictions of the world and to which we can unite ourselves through a growing universal and spiritual or a transcendental ecstasy."

Sri Aurobindo, The Synthesis of Yoga, Part Three: The Yoga of Divine Love, Chapter 7, The Ananda Brahman, pp. 568-569

Becoming a Conscious Human Expression of the Divine Nature

The various experiences of divine bliss that come to the seeker along the path of Yoga are considered to be "peak experiences" and they tend to come for a brief time, uplift the being, and then depart again. Amidst all the efforts, the struggles, the setbacks and the slow progress along the way, they are shining beacons that give the seeker a taste of what the spiritual evolution is leading towards, and encourages the patience and persistence needed to eventually reach the goal of transformation. Sri Aurobindo, however, is unwilling to accept the occasional and partial nature of these experiences as the sole possible result; rather, he believes that the entire life can be so transformed that it actually can live with this experience, and thereby become a conscious human expression of the divine nature of bliss.

"But the very spirit of Yoga is this, to make the exceptional normal, and to turn that which is above us and greater than our normal selves into our own constant consciousness. Therefore we should not hesitate to open ourselves more steadily to whatever experience of the Infinite we have, to purify and intensify it, to make it our object of constant thought and contemplation, till it becomes the originating power that acts in us, the Godhead we adore and embrace, our whole being is put into tune with it and it is made the very self of our being."

The normal physical, vital, emotional and mental nature from which we start is not tuned to hold this experience either for any great length of time, or to any great level of intensity. Thus, part of the process is to continually work on these instruments until they are able to receive, calibrate, and hold the experience. "Our experience of it has to be purified of any mental alloy in it, otherwise it departs, we cannot hold it. And part of this purification is that it shall cease to be dependent on any cause or exciting condition of the mind; it must become its own cause and self-existent, source of all other delight, which will exist only by it, and not attached to any cosmic or other image or symbol through which we first came into contact with it. Our experience of it has to be constantly intensified and made more concentrated; otherwise we shall only reflect it in the mirror of the imperfect mind and not reach that point of uplifting and transfiguration by which we are carried beyond the mind into the ineffable bliss."

"If we wait upon it for the inspiration of all our inner and outer acts, it will become the joy of the Divine pouring itself through us in light and love and power on life and all that lives. Sought by the adoration and love of the soul, it reveals itself as the Godhead, we see in it the face of God and know the bliss of our Lover. Tuning our whole being to it, we grow into a happy perfection of likeness to it, a human rendering of the divine nature. And when it becomes in every way the self of our self, we are fulfilled in being and we bear the plenitude."

Sri Aurobindo, The Synthesis of Yoga, Part Three: The Yoga of Divine Love, Chapter 7, The Ananda Brahman, pp. 569-570

The Revelation of the Divine Within Ourselves

The seeker may experience the Brahman, the Divine Consciousness within himself, just as he may experience the Brahman in the universal manifestation or in the transcendent that exceeds and is independent of the entire manifestation, individual and universal.

Within the individual seeker, there are several ways the Brahman may reveal himself, as Sri Aurobindo here describes: "Within us there are two centres of the Purusha, the inner Soul through which he touches us to our awakening; there is the Purusha in the lotus of the heart which opens upward all our powers and the Purusha in the thousand-petalled lotus whence descend through the thought and will, opening the third eye in us, the lightnings of vision and the fire of the divine energy. The bliss existence may come to us through either one of these centres."

The experience of the heart-lotus opening brings about the following: "When the lotus of the heart breaks open, we feel a divine joy, love and peace expanding in us like a flower of light which irradiates the whole being. They can then unite themselves with their secret source, the Divine in our hearts, and adore him as in a temple; they can flow upwards to take possession of the thought and the will and break out upward towards the Transcendent; they stream out in thought and feeling and act towards all that is around us."

This experience comes and goes as long as there are parts of the being that put up any resistance, and it is thus necessary to undertake patient and persistent effort of purification and concentration to make the experience constant and all-pervasive in the being.

"When the upper lotus opens, the whole mind becomes full of a divine light, joy and power, behind which is the Divine, the Lord of our being on his throne with our soul beside him or drawn inward into his rays; all the thought and will become then a luminosity, power and ecstasy; in communication with the Transcendent, this can pour down towards our mortal members and flow by them outwards on the world."

This experience, too, is subject to variations due to the inability of the instrument to hold and fix the intensity for long periods of time without break. "…but as we grow in the power to hold this new existence, we become able to look long on the sun from which this irradiation proceeds and in our inner being we can grow one body with it."

The poise of the seeker can also aid in the process. "Sometimes the rapidity of this change depends on the strength of our longing for the Divine thus revealed, and on the intensity of our force of seeking; but at others it proceeds rather by a passive surrender to the rhythms of his all-wise working which acts always by its own at first inscrutable method. But the latter becomes the foundation when our love and trust are complete and our whole being lies in the clasp of a Power that is perfect love and wisdom."

Sri Aurobindo, The Synthesis of Yoga, Part Three: The Yoga of Divine Love, Chapter 7, The Ananda Brahman, pp. 570-571

The Revelation of the Divine
In the World Around Us

The Upanishads reveal the universal Presence of the Divine in all existences. The Isha Upanishad begins with this insight: "All this is for habitation by the Lord, whatsoever is individual universe of movement in the universal motion." (Sri Aurobindo, *The Upanishads*, Isha Upanishad, v. 1, pg. 19)

But the Isha Upanishad is not alone in describing the universality of the Divine. The Shwetashwatara Upanishad declares: "That alone is the fire and That the sun and That the wind and That too the moon; That is the Luminous, That the Brahman, That the waters, That the Father and Lord of creatures. Thou art the woman and Thou the man; Thou art a boy and again a young virgin; Thou art yonder worn and aged man that walkest bent with thy staff. Lo, Thou becomest born and the world is full of thy faces. Thou art the blue bird and the green and the scarlet-eyed, the womb of lightning and the seasons and the oceans. Thou art that which is without beginning and Thou movest with Thy pervasive extension whence all the worlds are born. (op. cit, Shwetashwatara Upanishad, ch. 4, v. 2-4, pg. 369)

Sri Aurobindo expounds: "The Divine reveals himself in the world around us when we look upon that with a spiritual desire of delight that seeks him in all things. There is often a sudden opening by which the veil of forms is itself turned into a revelation. A universal spiritual Presence, a universal peace, a universal infinite Delight has manifested, immanent, embracing, all-penetrating. This Presence by our love of it, our delight in it, our constant thought of it returns and grows upon us; it becomes the thing that we see and all else is only its habitation, form and symbol. Even all that is most outward, the body, the form, the sound, whatever our senses seize, are seen as this Presence; they cease to be physical and are changed into a substance of spirit."

The result of an ever-increasing identification with this experience is to transform our consciousness and our existence into a manifestation of the Divine in the universal creation.

"Our own mind, life, body become to us only its habitation and temple, a form of its working and an instrument of its self-expression. All is only soul and body of this delight."

As Sri Aurobindo poetically states in his epic poem, Savitri: A Legend and a Symbol: "and Matter shall reveal the Spirit's face."

Sri Aurobindo, The Synthesis of Yoga, Part Three: The Yoga of Divine Love, Chapter 7, The Ananda Brahman, pg. 571

The Revelation and Realisation of the Transcendent Divine Presence

There is not a single way for everyone to experience the Divine Presence. Some experience the Divine within, some in the universal manifestation, and still others experience the Divine as an infinite and abstract Presence beyond all the forms of the manifested universe, above and outside us. It is quite common for people to describe the Divine as a Presence residing in a heaven above, separate and independent of us and of everything else in the world. The traditional Yoga of knowledge seeks to dissasociate the individual from the manifestation in order to obtain unity with this transcendent, infinite, immutable divine Presence.

Sri Aurobindo observes: "We see or feel him as a high-uplifted Presence, a great infinite of Ananda above us,–or in it, our Father in heaven,–and do not feel or see him in ourselves or around us. So long as we keep this vision, the mortality in us quelled by that Immortality; it feels the light, power and joy and responds to it according to its capacity; or it feels the descent of the spirit and it is then for a time transformed or else uplifted into some lustre of reflection of the light and power; it becomes a vessel of the Ananda."

It is difficult, if not actually impossible, for the human instrument to hold this greater light, force and bliss continuously. "But at other times it lapses into the old mortality and exists or works dully or pettily in the ruck of its earthly habits. The complete redemption comes by the descent of the divine Power into the human mind and body and the remoulding of their inner life into the divine image,–what the Vedic seers called the birth of the Son by the sacrifice. It is in fact by a continual sacrifice or offering, a sacrifice of adoration and aspiration, of works, of though and knowledge, of the mounting flame of the Godward will that we build ourselves into the being of this Infinite."

Sri Aurobindo, The Synthesis of Yoga, Part Three: The Yoga of Divine Love, Chapter 7, The Ananda Brahman, pp. 571-572

The Fullness of Consciousness of the Ananda Brahman

As the experience deepens, the seeker integrates the awareness of the Ananda Brahman within, around and above. Sri Aurobindo observes: "When we possess firmly this consciousness of the Ananda Brahman in all of these three manifestations, above, within, around, we have the full oneness of it and embrace all existences in its delight, peace, joy and love; then all the worlds become the body of this self."

At this point, there is no wall of division that creates the illusion of complete separateness and difference between the individual and the world and the Divine transcendent consciousness. There is a recognition that all is One. "The Spirit who is here in a man and the Spirit who is there in the Sun, it is one Spirit and there is no other." (Sri Aurobindo, *The Upanishads,* Taittiriya Upanishad, Brahmanandavalli ch. 8, pg. 273)

Sri Aurobindo cautions, however, that it is not a fully complete awareness and experience if this is an impersonal realisation only. "But we have not richest knowledge of this Ananda if it is only an impersonal presence, largeness or immanence that we feel, if our adoration has not been intimate enough for this Being to reveal to us out of its wide-extended joy the face and body and make us feel the hands of the Friend and Lover. Its impersonality is the blissful greatness of the Brahman, but from that can look out upon us the sweetness and intimate control of the divine Personality. For Ananda is the presence of the Self and Master of our being and the stream of its outflowing can be the pure joy of his Lila."

It is in the integration of the experience of Ananda in both the Impersonal and the Personal Divine that the seeker experiences the fullness of the consciousness of the Ananda Brahman.

Sri Aurobindo, The Synthesis of Yoga, Part Three: The Yoga of Divine Love, Chapter 7, The Ananda Brahman, pg. 572

Chapter Eight

The Mystery of Love

Love and the Experience of the Impersonal Divine

When we consider love as a motive force or an experience, we associate it with an object and with a personal relationship. Thus, we tend to disregard the idea that love can be active in relation to the Impersonal Brahman, and we tend to treat the seeking after the Impersonal as the province solely of the Yoga of knowledge, with an austere seeking that avoids the implications of the emotions or feelings of love.

Sri Aurobindo observes: "...for in the current forms of Yoga it is supposed that the Impersonal can only be sought for a complete unity in which God and our own person disappear and there is none to adore or to be adored; only the delight of the experience of oneness and infinity remains."

Looked at from the viewpoint of our mental logic, therefore, there is no place for devotion in that path. Sri Aurobindo reminds us however that spiritual experience exceeds the mental conceptions and limitations. "But in truth the miracles of spiritual consciousness are not to be subjected to so rigid a logic. When we first come to feel the presence of the infinite, as it is the finite personality in us which is touched by it, that may well answer to the touch and call with a sort of adoration. Secondly, we may regard the Infinite not so much as a spiritual status of oneness and bliss. or that only as its mould and medium of being, bur rather as the presence of the ineffable Godhead to our consciousness, and then too love and adoration find their place. And even when our personality seems to disappear into unity with it, it may still be–and really is–the individual divine who is melting to the universal or the supreme by a union in which love and lover and loved are forgotten in a fusing experience of ec-stasy, but are still there latent in the oneness and subconsciently persisting in it. All union of the self by love must necessarily be of this nature. We may even say, in a sense, that it is to have this joy of union as the ultimate crown of all the varied experiences of spiritual relation between the individual soul and God that the One became many in the universe."

Sri Aurobindo, The Synthesis of Yoga, Part Three: The Yoga of Divine Love, Chapter 8, The Mystery of Love, pg. 573

The Integral Devotion: Transcendent, Universal and Individual

The practitioners of the Yoga of knowledge, even in their seeking of the Absolute, may find that they are brought face to face with the Divine Personality, since there is no real separation that divides the Impersonal from the Personal aspect of the Divine. The Impersonal maintains the characteristics of Sat (Existence), Chit (Consciousness) and Ananda (Bliss) and thus, while not being limited by the names and forms in the universal creation, the Impersonal certainly contains, embodies and encompasses them.

Sri Aurobindo comments: "The Divine is a Being and not an abstract existence or a status of pure timeless infinity; the original and universal existence is He, but that existence is inseparable from consciousness and bliss of being, and an existence conscious of its own being and its own bliss is what we may well call a divine infinite Person,–Purusha. Moreover all consciousness implies power, Shakti; where there is infinite consciousness of being, there is infinite power of being, and by that power all exists in the universe. All beings exist in this Being; all things are the faces of God; all thought and action and feeling and love proceed from him and return to him, all their results have him for source and support and secret goal."

With this understanding, we may then understand the nature of the devotion of the seeker in the integral Yoga: "It is to this Godhead, this Being that the Bhakti of an integral Yoga will be poured out and uplifted. Transcendent, it will seek him in the ecstasy of an absolute union; universal, it will seek him in infinite quality and every aspect and in all beings with a universal delight and love; individual, it will enter into all human relations with him that love creates between person and person."

Sri Aurobindo, The Synthesis of Yoga, Part Three: The Yoga of Divine Love, Chapter 8, The Mystery of Love, pp. 573-574

Approaching God Through
Our Limited Human Nature

For the practitioner of the Integral Yoga, an all-encompassing devotion is the eventual result. Each person, however, takes up their spiritual practice and focus based on the pre-existing conditions and development of their individual nature within the context of their society, education and background. For the most part, this leads to a more narrow focus initially on a particular aspect, attribute or form of the Divinity. Even in the normal life, not focused on Yoga, there are specific developed qualities and experiences which, over time, are intended to broaden and open the individual to a wider understanding and basis, which represents a preparation for the development of a spiritual life.

Sri Aurobindo observes, with regard to the comprehensive approach needed for the integral Yoga: "in fact, it is only possible if the intelligence, the temperament, the emotional mind have already been developed into largeness and fineness by the trend of our previous living. That is what the experience of the normal life is meant to lead to by its widening culture of the intellect, the aesthetic and emotional mind and of our parts too of will and active experience. it widens and refines the normal being so that it may open easily to all the truth of That which was preparing it for the temple of its self-manifestation. Ordinarily, man is limited in all these parts of his being and he can grasp at first only so much of the divine truth as has large correspondence to his own nature and its past development and associations. Therefore God meets us first in different limited affirmations of his divine qualities and nature; he presents himself to the seeker as an absolute of the things he can understand and to which his will and heart can respond; he discloses some name and aspect of his Godhead. This is what is called in Yoga the *ista-devata*, the name and form elected by our nature for its worship."

This leads naturally to the many forms of God that are worshipped by people all over the world. "These are those forms of Vishnu, Shiva, Krishna, Kali, Durga, Christ, Buddha, which the mind of man seizes on for adoration. Even the monotheist who worships a formless Godhead, yet gives to him some form of quality, some mental form or form of Nature by which he envisages and approaches him. But to be able to see a living form, a mental body, as it were, of the Divine gives to the approach a greater closeness and sweetness."

Sri Aurobindo, The Synthesis of Yoga, Part Three: The Yoga of Divine Love, Chapter 8, The Mystery of Love, pp. 574-575

The Way of Devotion in the Integral Yoga

The integral Yoga accepts the reality of the world and our individual existence as a manifestation of the Divine. There is no ultimate break between the "reality" of the Divine and the "illusion" of the world. In a traditional practice of devotional Yoga, concentration is placed on the specific form of the Godhead, and a relationship of adoration is established between the practitioner and the Divine form. In the integral Yoga, however, the devotion must break through all the limitations and see, experience, relate to and adore God in oneself, in the universal manifestation and in the Transcendent which exceeds all the specific names and forms of the manifestation while still encompassing them.

Sri Aurobindo explains further: "The way of the integral Yoga of Bhakti will be to universalise this conception of the Deity, to personalise him intimately by a multiple and an all-embracing relation, to make him constantly present to all the being and to devote, give up, surrender the whole being to him, so that he shall dwell near to us and in us and we with him and in him.....a constant thinking of him in all things and seeing of him always and everywhere is essential to this way of devotion. When we look on the things of physical Nature, in them we have to see the divine object of our love; when we look upon men and beings, we have to see him in them and in our relation with them to see that we are entering into relations with forms of him; when breaking beyond the limitation of the material world we know or have relations with the beings of other planes, still the same thought and vision has to be made real to our minds."

In our normal everyday view of things, we see each individual and each physical form or object as something separate and distinct, and we do not ordinarily see and recognize the divinity that is expressed there. We then treat the Divine as someone or something abstract or at least different from the forms and forces and personalities we see in the world. The integral seeker corrects this misperception with the higher insight that the Upanishads relate "All this is the Brahman."

"In all godheads we have to see this one God whom we worship with our heart and all our being; they are forms of his divinity.

So enlarging our spiritual embrace we reach a point at which all is he and the delight of this consciousness becomes to us our normal uninterrupted way of looking at the world. That brings us the outward or objective universality of our union with him."

Sri Aurobindo, The Synthesis of Yoga, Part Three: The Yoga of Divine Love, Chapter 8, The Mystery of Love, pp. 575-576

Developing a Constant Inner Communion Is Key to Transforming the Life

Because the integral Yoga takes up all of life, the seeker cannot rest content with a sense of union, adoration or joy that comes through abandonment or renunciation of the outer life of action in the world. Sri Aurobindo describes "a constant inner communion" as the leverage to begin to transform all one's thoughts, feelings and actions into an expression of the Divine.

"All our thoughts, impulses, feelings, actions have to be referred to him for his sanction or disallowance, or if we cannot yet reach this point, to be offered to him in our sacrifice of aspiration, so that he may more and more descend into us and be present in them all and pervade them with all his will and power, his light and knowledge, his love and delight. In the end all our thoughts, feelings, impulses, actions will begin to proceed from him and change into some divine seed and form of themselves; in our whole inner living we shall have grown conscious of ourselves as a part of his being till between the existence of the Divine whom we adore and our own lives there is no longer any division. So too in all happenings we have to come to see the dealings with us of the divine Lover and take such pleasure in them that even grief and suffering and physical pain become his gifts and turn to delight and disappear finally into delight, slain by the sense of the divine contact, because the touch of his hands is the alchemist of a miraculous transformation. Some reject life because it is tainted with grief and pain, but to the God-lover grief and pain become means of meeting with him, imprints of his pressure and finally cease as soon as our union with his nature becomes too complete for these masks of the universal delight at all to conceal it. They change into the Ananda."

Sri Aurobindo, The Synthesis of Yoga, Part Three: The Yoga of Divine Love, Chapter 8, The Mystery of Love, pg. 576

Devotion and Knowledge

Traditionally, the Yoga of devotion has been seen as separate from the Yoga of knowledge, and as leading to a different resolution of the spiritual quest. The integral Yoga of Sri Aurobindo acknowledges that each traditional path of Yoga has its own starting point based in different aspects of the human being, but at a certain point in the process, each path can merge into a more comprehensive approach and bring forth the fruits of the other paths.

Sri Aurobindo describes the development of knowledge from a starting point of devotion: "That which in the end contains, takes up or unifies them all, is the relation of lover and beloved, because that is the most intense and blissful of all and carries up all the rest into its heights and yet exceeds them. He is the teacher and guide and leads us to knowledge; at every step of the developing inner light and vision, we feel his touch like that of the artist moulding our clay of mind, his voice revealing the truth and its word, the thought he gives us to which we respond, the flashing of his spears of lightning which chase the darkness of our ignorance. Especially, in proportion as the partial lights of our mind become transformed into lights of gnosis, in whatever slighter or greater degree that may happen, we feel it as a transformation of our mentality into his and more and more he becomes the thinker and seer in us. We cease to think and see for ourselves, but think only what he wills to think for us and see only what he sees for us. And then the teacher is fulfilled in the lover; he lays hands on all our mental being to embrace and possess, to enjoy and use it."

Sri Aurobindo, The Synthesis of Yoga, Part Three: The Yoga of Divine Love, Chapter 8, The Mystery of Love, pp. 576-577

Devotion and Works

The underlying principle of the traditional Yoga of works is obedience to the Divine Will in works. This approach may, however, be one of long-suffering carrying of a burden if it is not modified by the spirit of love and devotion. It may also emphasize a difference between the Master and the servant which accentuates the apparent separation and division between the human being as instrument of divine action and the Divine Master who appoints the practitioner to the chosen effort.

Sri Aurobindo describes the modified relationship that can eventuate when the seeker approaches the way of works from the side of devotion: "He is the Master; but in this way of approach all distance and separation, all awe and fear and mere obedience disappear, because we become too close and united with him for these things to endure and it is the lover of our being who takes it up and occupies and uses and does with it whatever he wills. Obedience is the sign of the servant, but that is the lowest stage of this relation, *dasya*. Afterwards we do not obey, but move to his will as the string replies to the finger of the musician. To be the instrument is this higher stage of self-surrender and submission. But this is the living and loving instrument and it ends in the whole nature of our being becoming the slave of God, rejoicing in his possession and its own blissful subjection to the divine grasp and mastery. With a passionate delight it does all he wills it to do without questioning and bears all he would have it bear, because what it bears is the burden of the beloved being."

Sri Aurobindo, The Synthesis of Yoga, Part Three: The Yoga of Divine Love, Chapter 8, The Mystery of Love, pg. 577

Aspects of the Personal Relationship of the Seeker with the Divine

The relationship between the individual and the Divine is not limited to one particular form in the Yoga of love and devotion. There are a number of relations, any of which may be predominant at one time or another. They all enter into the complex and rich tapestry of love and intimacy which the human individual has with the Divine Personality. These aspects represent the deepening and widening of the Yoga of love and devotion.

Sri Aurobindo observes: "He is the friend, the adviser, helper, saviour in trouble and distress, the defender from enemies, the hero who fights our battles for us or under whose shield we fight, the charioteer, the pilot of our ways. And here we come at once to a closer intimacy; he is the comrade and eternal companion, the playmate of the game of living. But still there is so far a certain division, however pleasant, and friendship is too much limited by the appearance of beneficence. The lover can wound, abandon, be wroth with us, seem to betray, yet our love endures and even grows by these oppositions; they increase the joy of reunion and the joy of possession; through them the lover remains the friend, and all that he does, we find in the end, has been done by the lover and helper of our being for our soul's perfection as well as for his joy in us. These contradictions lead to a greater intimacy. He is the father and mother too of our being, its source and protector and its indulgent cherisher and giver of our desires. He is the child born to our desire whom we cherish and rear. All these things the lover takes up; his love in its intimacy and oneness keeps in it the paternal and maternal care and lends itself to our demands upon it. All is unified in that deepest many-sided relation."

Sri Aurobindo, The Synthesis of Yoga, Part Three: The Yoga of Divine Love, Chapter 8, The Mystery of Love, pp. 577-578

Love As the Central Foundation of Divine Realisation

Those who practice the traditional Yoga of devotion eventually reach a stage where the passionate and intense embrace of the Divine Lover is the central focus of their life and action. This element is also true for the seeker of the integral Yoga; however, the integral practitioner will naturally incorporate the elements of knowledge and works into his development. This implies a certain less intense and exclusive nature of the relationship of love, as these other elements claim time, attention and focus as well. The central foundation of the development of knowledge and works in the seeker who starts from love and devotion remains the intensity of the personal relationship developed through the aspect of love.

Sri Aurobindo elaborates: "The growing of the love of God must carry with it in him an expansion of the knowledge of God and of the action of the divine Will in his nature and living. The divine Lover reveals himself; he takes possession of the life. But still the essential relation will be that of love from which all things flow, love passionate, complete, seeking a hundred ways of fulfilment, every means of mutual possession, a million facets of the joy of union. All the distinctions of the mind, all its barriers and "cannot be"'s, all the cold analyses of the reason are mocked at by this love or they are only used as the tests and fields and gates of union. Love comes to us in many ways; it may come as an awakening to the beauty of the Lover, by the sight of an ideal face and image of him, by his mysterious hints to us of himself behind the thousand faces of things in the world, by a slow or sudden need of the heart, by a vague thirst in the soul, by the sense of someone near us drawing us or pursuing us with love or of someone blissful and beautiful whom we must discover."

We may even find that "...the lover whom we think not of, may pursue us, may come upon us in the midst of the world and seize on us for his own whether at first we will or no." All of the possible relations, including those of the enemy, may open the door for the development of love. All human emotions related to the experience of love, including stages of jealousy, confusion, misunderstanding, and feelings of abandonment or separation, may arise at one time or another in the process.

"We throw up all the passions of the heart against him, till they are purified into a sole ecstasy of bliss and oneness. ... Our higher and our lower members are both flooded with it [love], the mind and life no less than the soul: even the physical body takes its share of the joy, feels the touch, is filled in all its limbs, veins, nerves with the flowing of the wine of the ecstasy, *amrta*. Love and Ananda are the last word of being, the secret of secrets, the mystery of mysteries."

Sri Aurobindo, The Synthesis of Yoga, Part Three: The Yoga of Divine Love, Chapter 8, The Mystery of Love, pp. 578-579

The Way of Love and the Supreme Liberation

In the Bhagavad Gita, Sri Krishna declares the "supreme secret" to be total devotion to the Supreme in all ways and aspects of the being: "Become my-minded, my lover and adorer, a sacrificer to Me, bow thyself to Me, to Me thou shalt come, this is my pledge and promise to thee, for dear art thou to Me. Abandon all dharmas and take refuge in Me alone. I will deliver thee from all sin and evil, do not grieve." (Sri Aurobindo, *Bhagavad Gita and Its Message*, ch. 18, v. 65-66, pg. 286)

The way of the Bhakta is able to bring about the highest forms of liberation from the bondage of action. Sri Aurobindo elaborates: "Thus universalised, personalised, raised to its intensities, made all-occupying, all-embracing, all-fulfilling, the way of love and delight gives the supreme liberation."

"We have the absolute union of the divine with the human spirit…; in that reveals itself a content of all that depends here upon difference,–but there the difference is only a form of oneness,– Ananda too of nearness and contact and mutual presence,… Ananda of mutual reflection, the thing that we call likeness,…, and other wonderful things too for which language has as yet no name. There is nothing which is beyond the reach of the God-lover or denied to him; for he is the favourite of the divine Lover and the self of the Beloved."

Sri Aurobindo, The Synthesis of Yoga, Part Three: The Yoga of Divine Love, Chapter 8, The Mystery of Love, pg. 579

Conclusions

We have completed our review of the third section of Sri Aurobindo's *The Synthesis of Yoga*, focused on the Yoga of Love and Devotion, having previously reviewed the Yoga of Knowledge and the Yoga of Works. Each of the three primary paths of Yoga utilizes a particular capacity of the human being as the lever for the spiritual evolutionary action. Due to the differences in the capacity relied upon in each path, there is a different core focus and a different set of criteria for each one. We cannot say that any one of the three is "better" than the other two for spiritual realisation. In fact, a particular individual may find that there are various stages in the progress that call forth the focus and capacities of one or the other of these paths to achieve a particular step along the way.

Sri Aurobindo has clearly described the practice of the Yoga of love and devotion and has shown that someone starting with this path will eventually need to incorporate both knowledge and the will in works to achieve an integral development of the entire being and achieve unification, not only with the static, unmoving Impersonal but also with the Personal manifestation of the Divine. He has also described the power of this path to achieve complete realisation. Just as Sri Krishna in the Bhagavad Gita treats total devotion as the "supreme secret", Sri Aurobindo concurs and elaborates on this path in terms of the intensity and intimacy it develops as the seeker works to achieve union with the Divine in all ways and aspects of his being.

The fourth and final section of *The Synthesis of Yoga* takes up one of Sri Aurobindo's unique contributions to the science of Yoga when it focuses on the "Yoga of Self Perfection". That section builds upon the capacities of each of the traditional paths of Yoga to bring about a total transformation of the individual within the framework of the universal manifestation. The world is not treated as a pure "illusion" from which one needs to escape, but is treated as "reality omnipresent" that embodies the Divine in all names, forms and forces, and treats the individual as a unique aspect of this Divine manifestation.

Sri Aurobindo, The Synthesis of Yoga, Part Three: The Yoga of Divine Love, Conclusions

BIBLIOGRAPHY

Aurobindo, Sri. *Bhagavad Gita and Its Message.*
ISBN 978-0-9415-2478-0
Lotus Press, Twin Lakes, WI USA | www.lotuspress.com

Aurobindo, Sri. *Essays on the Gita.*
ISBN 978-0-9149-5518-4
Lotus Press, Twin Lakes, WI, USA | www.lotuspress.com

Aurobindo, Sri. *The Life Divine.*
ISBN 978-0-9415-2461-2
Lotus Press, Twin Lakes, WI, USA | www.lotuspress.com

Aurobindo, Sri. *The Synthesis of Yoga.*
ISBN 978-0-9415-2465-0
Lotus Press, Twin Lakes, WI, USA | www.lotuspress.com

Aurobindo, Sri. *The Upanishads.*
ISBN 978-0-9149-5523-8
Lotus Press, Twin Lakes, WI, USA | www.lotuspress.com

Lotus Press is the US publisher of the primary writings of Sri Aurobindo. Most of the major writings are now also available on the Amazon Kindle format. Amazon provides free kindle reading apps for PC, MAC, android, iphone, ipad and a number of other devices and platforms, as well as supporting the various Kindle reader devices they have made available. They are also available in Apple itunes, Kobo, Barnes & Noble/Nook, GooglePlay and KOBO platforms.

ABOUT THE AUTHOR:

Santosh Krinsky has been studying Sri Aurobindo's *The Life Divine* since he was introduced to it in 1971. After residing at Sri Aurobindo Ashram in India for part of 1973-1974, he returned to the USA where he has been involved in the distribution and eventually the publication of the major writings of Sri Aurobindo. In 1981 he founded Lotus Light Publications which eventually became Lotus Press and took up the publication of the writings of Sri M P Pandit as well as Sri Aurobindo. Lotus Press today is one of the leading publishers also in the field of Ayurveda and alternative healing modalities, including Reiki, as well as being the US publisher of Sri Aurobindo's major works.

Santosh is also one of the founders and currently the President of a non-profit organization The Institute for Wholistic Education. The Institute is dedicated to the work of integrating spirituality into daily life. Activities include various classes, meditations, and sponsoring online informational websites and blog posts. The Institute also maintains a library of more than 6000 volumes available for use by seekers and interested parties who visit the center in Wisconsin.

Santosh and his wife Karuna reside in Racine, Wisconsin.

For more information about the work you can visit the following websites:

Sri Aurobindo Information:
www.aurobindo.net

Sri M.P. Pandit Information:
www.mppandit.com

Institute for Wholistic Education:
www.wholisticinstitute.org

Lotus Press:
www.lotuspress.com

Sri Aurobindo Studies blog:
http://sriaurobindostudies.wordpress.com

Daily Twitter feed on Sri Aurobindo and Ayurveda:
www.twitter.com/santoshk1

ABOUT THE AUTHOR:

SRI AUROBINDO

Sri Aurobindo was born in Calcutta on 15 August 1872. At the age of seven he was taken to England for education. There he studied at St. Paul's School, London, and at King's College,

Cambridge. Returning to India in 1893, he worked for the next thirteen years in the Princely State of Baroda in the service of the Maharaja and as a professor in Baroda College. During this

period he also joined a revolutionary society and took a leading role in secret preparations for an uprising against the British Government in India.

In 1906, soon after the Partition of Bengal, Sri Aurobindo quit his post in Baroda and went to Calcutta, where he soon became one of the leaders of the Nationalist movement. He was the first political leader in India to openly put forward, in his newspaper Bande Mataram, the idea of complete independence for the country. Prosecuted twice for sedition and once for conspiracy, he was released each time for lack of evidence.

Sri Aurobindo had begun the practice of Yoga in 1905 in Baroda. In 1908 he had the first of several fundamental spiritual realisations. In 1910 he withdrew from politics and went to Pondicherry in order to devote himself entirely to his inner spiritual life and work. During his forty years in Pondicherry he evolved a new method of spiritual practice, which he called the Integral Yoga. Its aim is a spiritual realisation that not only liberates man's consciousness but also transforms his nature. In 1926, with the help of his spiritual collaborator, the Mother, he founded the Sri Aurobindo Ashram. Among his many writings are The Life Divine, The Synthesis of Yoga and Savitri. Sri Aurobindo left his body on 5 December 1950.

Major writings of Sri Aurobindo are published in the USA by Lotus Press, Twin Lakes, WI | www.lotuspress.com

TITLES BY SRI AUROBINDO

Bases of Yoga (New US Edition)	P	$6.95
Bhagavad Gita and Its Message	P	$15.95
Dictionary of Sri Aurobindo's Yoga (Compiled)	P	$13.95
Essays on the Gita (New US Edition)	P	$19.95
The Future Evolution of Man	P	$8.95
Gems from Sri Aurobindo, 2nd Series (Compiled)	P	$12.95
Gems from Sri Aurobindo, 3rd Series (Compiled)	P	$10.95
Gem from Sri Aurobindo, 4th Series (Compiled)	P	$8.95
Growing Within	P	$9.95
Human Cycle: Psychology of Social Development (New US Edition)	P	$14.95
Hymns to the Mystic Fire (New US Edition)	P	$17.95
Ideal of Human Unity (New US Edition)	P	$17.95
Integral Yoga: Sri Aurobindo's Teaching and Method of Practice (Compiled)	P	$14.95
The Life Divine (New US Edition)	P	$29.95
	HB	$39.95
Lights on Yoga	P	$3.95
Living Within (Compiled)	P	$8.95
Looking from Within (Compiled)	P	$6.95
The Mother (New US Edition)	P	$3.95
The Psychic Being: Soul in Evolution (Compiled)	P	$8.95
Rebirth and Karma (New US Edition)	P	$9.95
Savitri: A Legend and a Symbol (New US Edition)	P	$24.95
The Secret of the Veda (New US Edition)	P	$19.95
The Synthesis of Yoga (New US Edition)	P	$29.95
	HB	$34.95
The Upanishads (New US Edition)	P	$17.95
Wisdom of the Gita, 2nd Series (Compiled)	P	$10.95

Available from your local bookseller or
LOTUS PRESS, Box 325, Twin Lakes, WI 53181 USA
262/889-8561 • www.LotusPress.com
Email: lotuspress@lotuspress.com